# Great Creatures of the World

# SHARKS

Facts On File

New York • Oxford • Sydney

Sharks
A Great Creatures of the World book

Written by Sheena and Robert Coupe

Adapted from material supplied by:

Dr Leonard J.V. Compagno, senior research scientist, J.L.B. Smith Institute of Ichthyology, Grahamstown, South Africa
Carson Creagh BSc, editor and natural history writer, Sydney, New South Wales, Australia
Dr Guido Dingerkus, director, Natural History Consultants, Goshen, New York, USA
Hugh Edwards, marine photographer and author, Perth, Western Australia
Richard Ellis MA, marine artist and author, New York, USA
Dr Edward S. Hodgson, professor of biology, Tufts University, Medford, Massachusetts, USA
Roland Hughes BSc, former editor, *Australian Natural History*, Sydney, New South Wales, Australia
Dr C. Scott Johnson, research scientist, Biological Services Branch, Naval Ocean Systems Center, San Diego, California, USA
Dr John G. Maisey, associate curator, Department of Vertebrate Paleontology, American Museum of Natural History, New York, USA
Dr Arthur A. Myrberg Jr, professor of marine science, Rosenstiel School of Marine and Atmospheric Sciences, University of Miami, Miami, Florida, USA
A. M. Olsen MSc, former chief fisheries officer, Department of Agriculture and Fisheries, Adelaide, South Australia
Larry J. Paul BSc (Hons), Fisheries Research Centre, MAFFish Ministry of Agriculture and Fisheries, Wellington, New Zealand
Marty Snyderman, marine photographer, cinematographer and author, San Diego, California, USA
Dr John D. Stevens, senior research scientist, Division of Fisheries, CSIRO Marine Laboratories, Hobart, Tasmania, Australia
Dr Leighton R. Taylor Jr, former director of public programs, California Academy of Sciences, San Francisco, California, USA
Ron and Valerie Taylor, marine photographers and authors, Sydney, New South Wales, Australia
Dr Timothy C. Tricas, research associate, Washington University School of Medicine, St Louis, Missouri, and Marine Biological Laboratory, Woods Hole, Massachusetts, USA

Library of Congress Cataloguing-in-Publication Data:

Coupe, Sheena M.
    Sharks/Sheena Coupe.
      p. cm. — (A Great creatures book)
    Includes index.
    Summary: Describes the physical characteristics, habits, and natural environment of sharks and discusses their evolution and relationship with human beings.
    ISBN 0-8160-2270-4:
    1. Sharks — Juvenile literature. [1. Sharks] I. Title. II. Series.
QL638.9.C65 1990                        89-34671
597'.31—dc20                               CIP
                                            AC

British CIP data available on request

Produced by Weldon Owen Pty Limited
43 Victoria Street, McMahons Point, NSW 2060, Australia
Telex AA 23038  Fax (02) 929 8352
A member of the Weldon International Group of Companies
Sydney • San Francisco • Hong Kong • London • Chicago

Publisher: John Owen
Publishing Manager: Stuart Laurence
Managing Editor: Beverley Barnes
Project Coordinator: Sheena Coupe
Editor: Claire Craig
Designer: Diane Quick
Maps: Greg Campbell
Illustrations: Tony Pyrzakowski
Production Director: Mick Bagnato

Typeset by Keyset Phototype
Printed by Kyodo-Shing Loong Printing Industries
Printed in Singapore

10 9 8 7 6 5 4 3 2 1

*Page 1: A blacktip reef shark rests during the day beneath a ledge covered with coral.*

*Page 2: Tiger sharks are among the most efficient hunters in tropical waters.*

*Opposite page: The oceanic whitetip shark is very widespread in tropical regions.*

# Contents

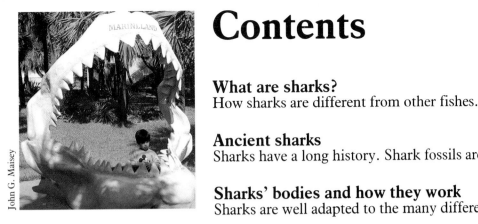

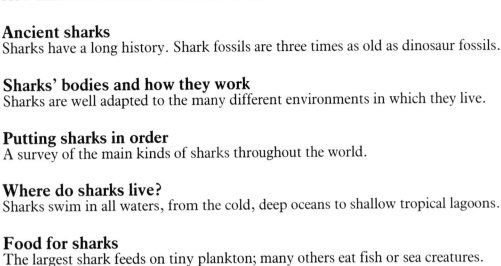

*Opposite page: The blue shark sometimes attacks survivors of shipwrecks and plane crashes.*

# What are sharks?

Many people fear them, but few people understand them. They can be eight times as large as a human being or so small that they will fit into your hand. Here we look at what makes sharks different from other fish.

When people think about sharks, they usually imagine large, hungry, sharp-toothed creatures that are constantly in search of human prey. This frightening image comes from the great publicity given to the rare cases of shark attack on humans and the way sharks are represented in sensational movies and books. For many people who have seen movies such as *Jaws*, the word "shark" brings to mind an enormous white pointer or "great white." But most sharks are not like this.

## Sharks and bony fishes

Like other fish and ocean-dwelling mammals, sharks are *vertebrates*. In other words, they have backbones. Most of the animals that swim in the world's oceans are known as bony fishes because they have skeletons of hard bone. Sharks' skeletons are made up of *cartilage*, which is strong and tough, but lighter and more elastic than bone. There are more than 20,000 species of bony fishes, but only about 350 species of sharks.

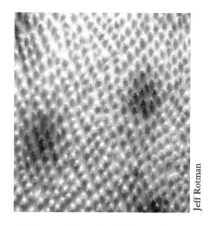

Jeff Rotman

▲ *These scales, or* denticles, *make a shark's fin feel rough if you touch it.*

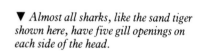

▲ *Goblin shark*

▼ *Almost all sharks, like the sand tiger shown here, have five gill openings on each side of the head.*

## The world's ugliest shark?

It depends on your point of view, but the goblin shark has been described as the ugliest of all sharks. Its long snout, which sticks out like a dagger blade above its beak-like upper jaw, certainly gives it a weird appearance. As its shape suggests, the goblin shark is a slow swimmer. It lives near the bottom of the ocean in most parts of the world and grows to almost 12 feet (3.6 m) long.

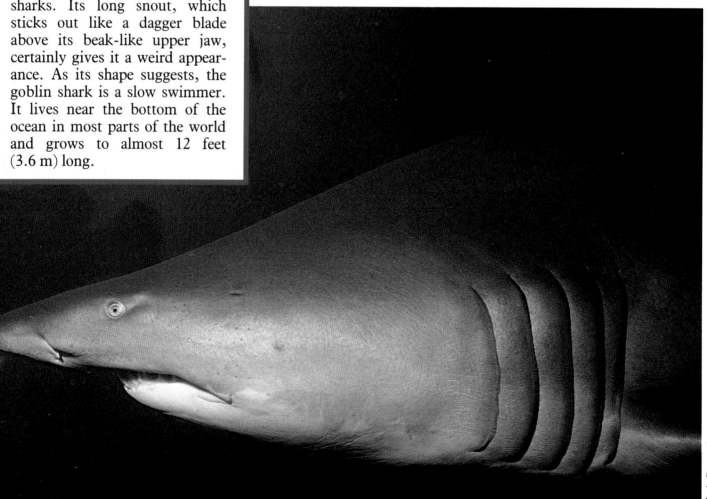

Kevin Deacon/Auscape

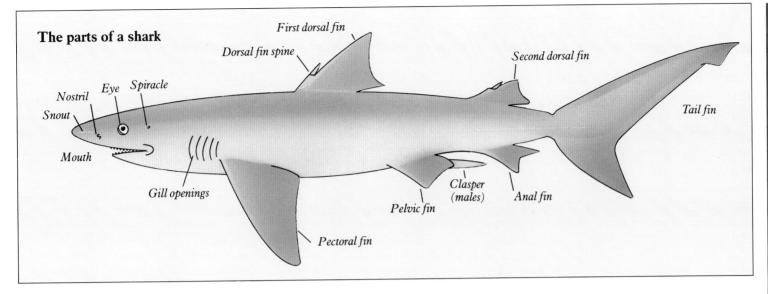

**The parts of a shark**

Snout · Nostril · Eye · Spiracle · Mouth · Gill openings · Dorsal fin spine · First dorsal fin · Second dorsal fin · Tail fin · Clasper (males) · Anal fin · Pelvic fin · Pectoral fin

▲ *In this diagram the main parts of a shark are labeled. It is important to understand that not all sharks have all these parts. Not all sharks, for example, have more than one dorsal fin, and most sharks have no spines on these dorsal fins. Just under one-third of shark species have no anal fin. The clasper is the male's reproductive organ.*

▼ *The pupil of the nurse shark's eye quickly becomes smaller as the shark swims from dark to light places.*

### Hunters of the sea

The great majority of sharks feed on other sea animals. Most sharks feed on particular species of marine life and will not usually eat anything that happens to turn up.

We usually think of sharks as solitary hunters, and this is true of large sharks like tiger sharks or great whites. Many other shark species, however, spend at least some of their time hunting in groups. Even for sharks, food is not always easy to find, and it is possible that in groups sharks have a better chance of locating the kind of food they are looking for.

Sharks and bony fishes are similar in many ways. They both breathe through gills that are situated at the sides of their heads; they often have very similar body shapes; and their bodies are covered with scales. However, there are also important differences between sharks and bony fishes. Sharks have between five and seven *gill* openings on each side of the head, while bony fishes have only one. Sharks' scales (called *denticles*) are tooth-like and much thicker than the transparent skinlike scales of bony fishes. The upper part of a shark's tail is larger than the lower part.

# Ancient sharks

Sharks have swum in the oceans of the world for more than 100 times as long as humans have lived on the earth. Scientists have been able to determine that the earliest sharks existed more than 450 million years ago. These ancient sharks were very different from the sharks of today.

### Tracing the history of sharks

What we know about the evolution of sharks through the ages is the result of the study of fossils that have been found in different parts of the world. Fossils can be either actual pieces of bone or teeth that have survived for great periods of time, or impressions in rocks that have formed over millions of years. These rocks may once have been mud or soil, and they can show an imprint of part or perhaps even all of an animal's skeleton.

The most common shark fossils are teeth because sharks, unlike most other animals, can lose many thousands of teeth during their lives. As teeth fall out, new ones grow to replace them. Shark skeletons, on the other hand, are made up not of solid bone, but of tiny particles that break up and become scattered when the shark dies. As a result, ancient shark skeletons have been found only in places where they were quickly covered with mud and where they have remained almost completely undisturbed. The few complete shark fossils that have been discovered are important clues in tracing the history of sharks.

### Primitive sharks

More than 400 million years ago, during what we call the Paleozoic era, a great deal of what is now North America was covered with a shallow ocean. In this ocean lived a number of primitive sharks.

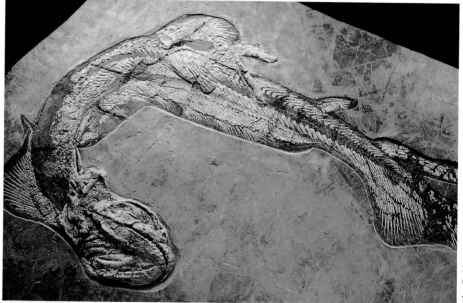

John G. Maisey

Ron & Valerie Taylor

John G. Maisey

▲ *A beautifully preserved fossil of a male xenacanth shark, which swam in rivers and lakes about 250 million years ago.*

◄ *The giant fossil teeth are from Carcharodon megalodon. The much smaller tooth is from a modern great white shark.*

▼ *The fossil remains of this Cladoselache, which are 400 million years old, were found in Tennessee in the southern United States.*

Skeletons of one of these sharks, called *Cladoselache*, have been found embedded in rocks in the north-central United States. *Cladoselache* was about 3 feet (1 m) long, and had long thin jaws and sharp thorny teeth. When scientists examined the fossils, they found that some of the fossils contained the skeletons of smaller fishes that seem to have been swallowed whole — and tail first. *Cladoselache* obviously did not chew all its food before swallowing it.

*Cladoselache* was probably a very swift swimmer that caught its prey on the move. It needed to move quickly to keep clear of the enormous armored fishes, six times its size, which lived in the same oceans.

Recent discoveries in various parts of the world indicate that many other primitive sharks, some protected by sharp bony spines, lived at the same time as *Cladoselache*.

## Xenacanths and hybodonts

During the Paleozoic era, a group of sharks began to live in freshwater environments all over the world. These sharks, now called xenacanths, grew to about 6 feet (2 m) long.

While xenacanths swam in the lakes and streams, another group of primitive sharks, now called hybodonts, began to live in the oceans about 320 million years ago. Unlike *Cladoselache*, these later sharks had low wide teeth, which they probably used for crushing shellfish.

The xenacanths disappeared about 220 million years ago. The hybodonts died out around the same time the dinosaurs disappeared from the earth — about 65 million years ago.

## Ancestors of modern sharks

The ancestors of most modern sharks can be traced back for only about 100 million years. Most of the evidence we have of these "modern" sharks consists of teeth. One species, *Carcharodon megalodon*, which lived about 20 million years ago, had enormous, rough-edged teeth that were more than 7 inches (18cm) long.

▼ *These rocks, discovered in Kansas in the north-central United States, show a very clear impression of a hybodont, an early shark.*

John G. Maisey

### Did you know?

Early this century scientists believed that the ancient shark *Carcharodon megalodon* grew almost 100 feet (30 m) long, but later discoveries have shown that it probably grew to only about 40 feet (12 m). This modern reconstruction of its jaws was based on a set of teeth discovered by Pete Harmatuk in North Carolina.

John G. Maisey

# Sharks' bodies and how they work

Sharks are well adapted to the environments in which they live. They have different body shapes and structures that allow them to live in different parts of the ocean and to move at speeds that are suited to their varying needs and feeding habits.

The diagram below shows three kinds of sharks. The shape of the sharks shown in the diagram is closely related to the part of the ocean they live in and how fast they move.

The whaler shark has the most typical body shape and more than half of all shark species have a shape similar to this. The slender, streamlined body helps the shark to move smoothly and swiftly through the water. The long upper part of its tail provides power as the shark swims in pursuit of its prey.

Mackerel sharks are rounder and fatter than the whaler sharks. Their cone-like shape helps them to cruise even more quickly than the whaler sharks.

Catsharks, on the other hand, are sluggish creatures that live near the bottom of the sea. They feed mainly on shellfish and other slow-moving prey. You can see from the diagram that they have a fairly large head, a long thin body and a small weak tail. They swim in wide curves, rather like eels.

## On the move

Sharks have fins (called *pectoral fins*) on the lower side of their bodies, at least one large dorsal fin on the middle of the back and a large tail fin. These fins, and the streamlined shape of their bodies, allow sharks to keep their balance as they swim through the water.

Sharks propel themselves through the water by moving their tails from one side to the other. They use their fins to slow them down, to speed up, to change direction, and to give them "lift" as they move forward.

The denticles of the faster-moving sharks are lighter and smaller than those of the slower species that stay near the sea bottom. This

▼ *The Tasmanian spotted catshark. Its name describes both its appearance and where it lives. It is typical of many catsharks whose colors allow them to blend well with their surroundings.*

Neville Coleman

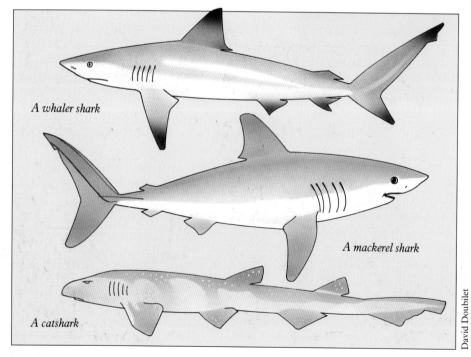

*A whaler shark*

*A mackerel shark*

*A catshark*

David Doubilet

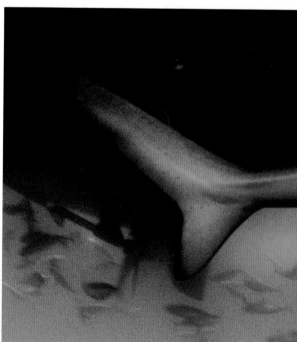

probably helps them to swim more quickly by reducing the amount of friction they cause. It is also possible that these denticles help sharks to swim more silently and to creep up on their unsuspecting prey.

**Q.** How long do sharks live?

**A.** The slower a shark grows, the longer it is likely to live. Most sharks live for between 20 and 30 years. The piked dogfish, which grows to only about 5 feet (1.6 m) long, holds the record. It lives for at least 40 years and some species may live for up to 100 years.

▼ *The great white shark (below) is a mackerel shark. It is rounder and fatter than a whaler shark. "Slender" and "streamlined" certainly describe the blue shark (bottom), a typical whaler shark. Like most sharks that swim swiftly in the open ocean, blue sharks have large eyes, which they use to search out their prey.*

## Colors and camouflage

Sharks also have a wide range of colors. Some of them are spectacularly beautiful; others look quite strange. Among the weirdest-looking sharks are the curiously named wobbegongs, or carpet sharks. These are large flat-bodied sharks with shaggy pieces of skin sticking out from the sides of the head. Their skin is blotchy to help camouflage them as they lie on coral reefs or sandy seabeds waiting for their prey. Some catsharks are also patterned for this reason.

## Breathing

Most sharks have five gill slits through which they take oxygen from the water as they swim. Water goes into the shark's mouth and over the gills, where the oxygen is pumped out and passed into the blood. Then the water comes out again through the gill slits.

When water becomes hot or polluted, it contains less oxygen. This is why sharks avoid areas of very warm water and often die when they are kept in captivity.

# Tails and teeth

Sharks' tails come in a great variety of shapes and sizes. The top part (or upper *lobe*) is almost always bigger than the bottom part (or lower lobe). This helps the shark swim efficiently. In other ways, sharks' tails vary according to where the sharks live and how active they are. Nurse sharks, for example, spend a lot of time on the sea floor. Their tails have only a tiny lower lobe, so they swim by moving their bodies from side to side rather like an eel. Great white sharks, on the other hand, have strong tails with the upper and lower lobes almost the same size. This helps the sharks to cruise through the water and also to make quick dashes after prey.

Sharks' teeth, too, come in assorted styles, depending on what the shark eats and how it catches its food. Some species have flat teeth with which they can crush shellfish, crabs, and lobsters. Others have sharp saw-edged teeth, which they use to cut up fish, squid, or octopuses. Sharks that grab fish and swallow them without chewing have sharp, spear-like teeth.

The pictures on these pages show some of the different kinds of shark teeth. It would be wise to keep away from all of them!

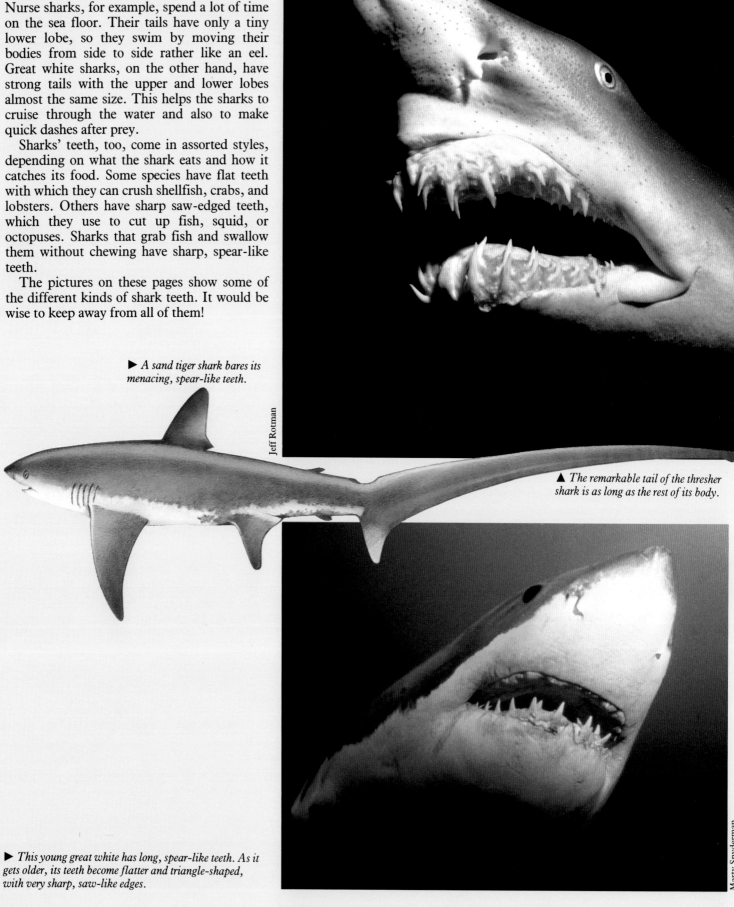

▶ *A sand tiger shark bares its menacing, spear-like teeth.*

Jeff Rotman

▲ *The remarkable tail of the thresher shark is as long as the rest of its body.*

▶ *This young great white has long, spear-like teeth. As it gets older, its teeth become flatter and triangle-shaped, with very sharp, saw-like edges.*

Marty Snyderman

▲ *Looking down on the spiky teeth of a sand tiger shark. These are suitable for holding fish, but not for chewing them.*

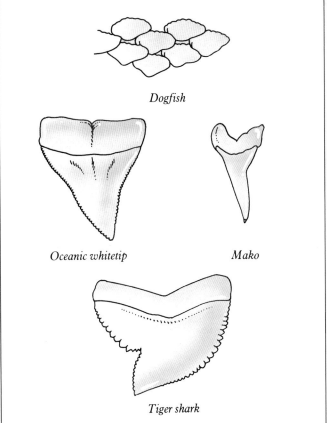

Dogfish

Oceanic whitetip

Mako

Tiger shark

▲ *Different tooth shapes are suited to catching and eating different types of food.*

▲ *Whaler sharks, such as tiger sharks and blue sharks, have jaws similar to these. They have sharp, saw-like teeth that allow them to catch and eat a great variety of marine life.*

◄ *If you really want to get inside a shark's mouth, this is the safest way to do it.*

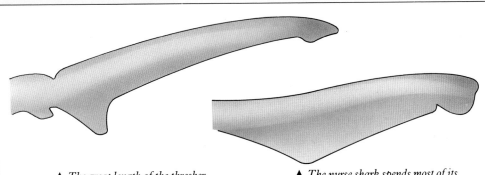
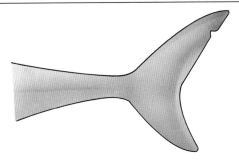

▲ *The great length of the thresher shark's tail does not slow it down. It moves quickly as it hunts for fish and squid, which it rounds up and then stuns with a quick, hard thump.*

▲ *The nurse shark spends most of its time on the sea bottom where it sleeps during the day. It sweeps its long tail from side to side as it moves along the sand in search of squid and shellfish.*

▲ *The tail of the great white is suited to both slow cruising and swift swoops on prey. Unlike many other sharks' tails, the lower lobe is almost as large as the upper lobe.*

# Putting sharks in order

There are more than 350 different kinds or species of sharks in waters all over the world. They have a wide variety of shapes, sizes, colors and habits.

The word "species" means "kind." Species that are related to each other can be put into larger groupings called "families." There are 30 families of sharks. Families with similar characteristics are put into still larger categories or "orders." There are eight orders of sharks.

In the following pages you will find information about the main characteristics of each order of sharks and illustrations of one or more sharks from each order. They will give you a good idea of just how many different kinds of sharks there are!

This system of organizing sharks starts from the most primitive sharks and goes through to the most highly developed.

## 1 Sixgill, sevengill and frilled sharks (Order Hexanchiformes)

There are five species of sharks in this group, and they are divided into two families. Members of these species have six or seven gill openings; other sharks have only five.

One of the families in this order contains only one species — the frilled shark. It is long and thin, and gets its name from the frilly edges around its six gill openings.

Members of this order are found all around the world, mainly in deep water, and can range in size from about 4.5 feet (1.4 m) to almost 17 feet (5 m) long. All members of this group give birth to young that are hatched inside the mother's body.

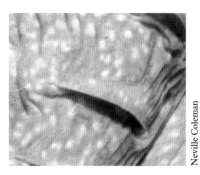

▲ *A close-up of a shark's gill slit. Water enters the shark's mouth, passes over the gills and then comes out again through the gill slits.*

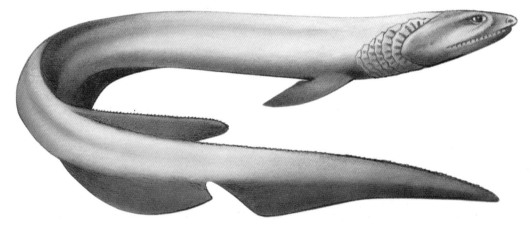

◄ *Frilled shark*

▼ *A spotted sevengill shark. The seven gill slits can be clearly seen just in front of its large pectoral fin.*

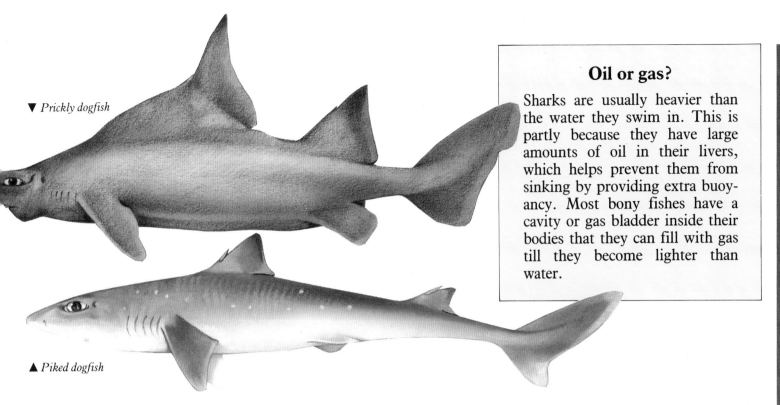

▼ *Prickly dogfish*

▲ *Piked dogfish*

## 2 Dogfish sharks
### (Order Squaliformes)

There are three families of dogfish sharks, containing 82 species. All members of this order have two dorsal fins and in many species these fins have sharp spines. You can see these spines very clearly in one of the illustrations above and the photograph below. Most dogfish sharks have sleek rounded bodies and long dog-like snouts.

All but six of the dogfish sharks belong to one very large family, which, a little confusingly, is known as the dogfish family. One of the illustrations shows a piked dogfish. It is possible that there are more piked dogfish than any other species of shark, and up to 27 million have been caught in a single year!

The prickly dogfish (top) belongs to a small family of five species, known as roughsharks. This name comes from the rough appearance created by the very high and jagged-looking dorsal fin.

Many dogfish sharks, including the piked dogfish, have very large livers that can weigh as much as a quarter of the shark's total weight. These livers contain oil that is rich in *squalene*, a compound widely used in the manufacture of cosmetics.

Dogfish sharks live in all the world's oceans, sometimes at very great depths. The young are hatched from eggs inside the mother's body. Although the majority of dogfish sharks grow to less than 3 feet (1 m) long, the piked dogfish can reach a length of 5 feet (1.6 m).

▼ *The shortnose spurdog, like the piked dogfish, has a liver that is a rich source of squalene. Because of the spines on its dorsal fins, this shark is also called "spiky Jack."*

Neville Coleman

## 3 Sawsharks
### (Order Pristiophoriformes)

It is clear from their appearance why these sharks are called sawsharks. There are about five species of these small sharks, and they all belong to one family.

Sawsharks live on the bottom of the ocean at moderate depths and are found mainly in waters where the temperature is between 50° and 70°F (10–20°C). They are harmless to humans but probably use the very sharp teeth that grow sideways from their snouts to injure their prey before they devour it. They eat small fish, shellfish, and squid.

▼ *Shortnose sawshark*

▼ *Angel shark*

▼ *Pacific angel shark*

Young sawsharks are born in litters of between five and twelve and will grow to between 2.5 feet and 4.5 feet (80–136 cm) long. While the young sharks are developing inside their mother's body, their sharp saw-like teeth are folded back so that they do not hurt the mother shark.

## 4 Angel sharks
### (Order Squatiniformes)

Angel sharks, with their flat bodies and large spreading fins, are unmistakable. Their tails, too, are different from those of other sharks — the bottom section (or lobe) is longer than the top section.

They live in moderate to warm waters around the world, but are usually found quite close to coastlines. They often spend their days half buried — and almost invisible — in the sandy or muddy bottom of the sea.

Angel sharks vary in length from about 22 to 79 inches (55–200 cm). The one shown above, called simply the angel shark, can grow to about 6 feet (1.8 m) long and is a favorite food in the Mediterranean region.

There are about 13 species of angel sharks, all belonging to the one family. Females produce litters of between 10 and 20 or more young sharks.

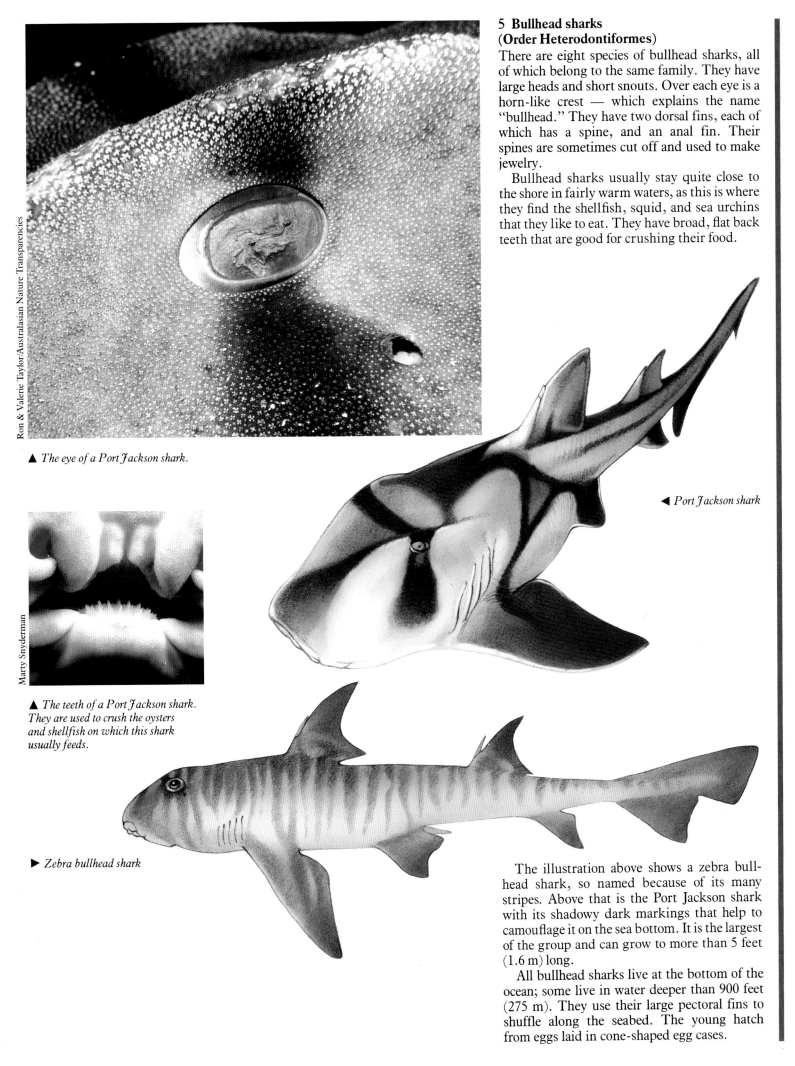

▲ *The eye of a Port Jackson shark.*

▲ *The teeth of a Port Jackson shark. They are used to crush the oysters and shellfish on which this shark usually feeds.*

▶ *Zebra bullhead shark*

## 5 Bullhead sharks
### (Order Heterodontiformes)

There are eight species of bullhead sharks, all of which belong to the same family. They have large heads and short snouts. Over each eye is a horn-like crest — which explains the name "bullhead." They have two dorsal fins, each of which has a spine, and an anal fin. Their spines are sometimes cut off and used to make jewelry.

Bullhead sharks usually stay quite close to the shore in fairly warm waters, as this is where they find the shellfish, squid, and sea urchins that they like to eat. They have broad, flat back teeth that are good for crushing their food.

◀ *Port Jackson shark*

The illustration above shows a zebra bullhead shark, so named because of its many stripes. Above that is the Port Jackson shark with its shadowy dark markings that help to camouflage it on the sea bottom. It is the largest of the group and can grow to more than 5 feet (1.6 m) long.

All bullhead sharks live at the bottom of the ocean; some live in water deeper than 900 feet (275 m). They use their large pectoral fins to shuffle along the seabed. The young hatch from eggs laid in cone-shaped egg cases.

## 6 Carpet sharks
### (Order Orectolobiformes)

This group of seven families and 33 species contains the world's largest fish — the huge but gentle whale shark, which grows to more than 39 feet (12 m) long — and the tiny and very rare barbelthroat carpet shark, which grows to just over 1 foot (33 cm).

All these sharks live in fairly warm locations in shallow to moderately deep water. They have two dorsal fins — but no spines — and small flaps of skin, or barbels, at the edges of their nostrils.

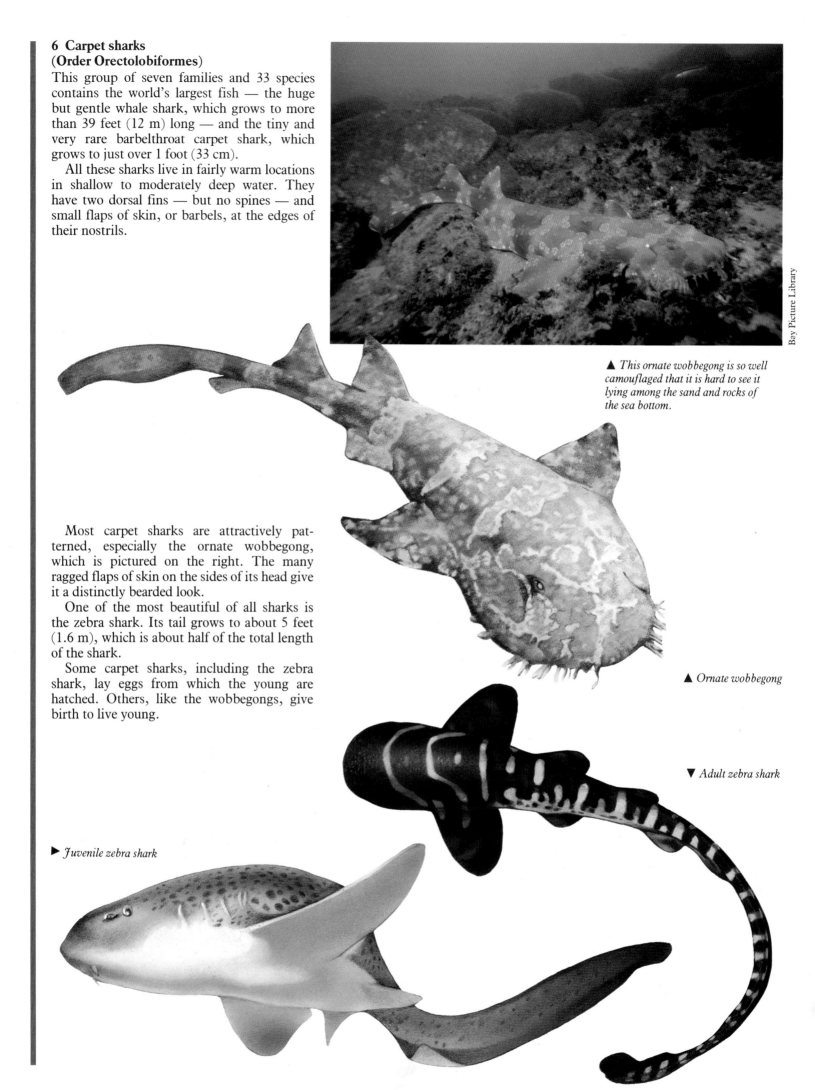

Bay Picture Library

▲ *This ornate wobbegong is so well camouflaged that it is hard to see it lying among the sand and rocks of the sea bottom.*

Most carpet sharks are attractively patterned, especially the ornate wobbegong, which is pictured on the right. The many ragged flaps of skin on the sides of its head give it a distinctly bearded look.

One of the most beautiful of all sharks is the zebra shark. Its tail grows to about 5 feet (1.6 m), which is about half of the total length of the shark.

Some carpet sharks, including the zebra shark, lay eggs from which the young are hatched. Others, like the wobbegongs, give birth to live young.

▲ *Ornate wobbegong*

▼ *Adult zebra shark*

▶ *Juvenile zebra shark*

## 7 Mackerel sharks
### (Order Lamniformes)

This group consists of about 15 species, which are spread over seven families. They are found all over the world, except in the very cold Arctic and Antarctic seas, and live in all depths of water.

All mackerel sharks, except one, grow to more than 10 feet (3 m) long. Both the largest and the smallest of them are notable for the size of their eyes. The enormous basking shark, which usually grows to about 32 feet (9.8 m), but which can be much larger, has tiny bead-like eyes that are hardly visible in its huge bulk. The crocodile shark grows to only about 3.6 feet (1.1 m) long, but has huge and conspicuous saucer-like eyes.

The shortfin mako is the fastest swimmer among the world's sharks. It belongs to the same family as the great white shark and is often hunted by big-game fishermen who have learned to respect its large, deadly teeth and aggressive manner.

All species of mackerel shark give birth to young that have hatched inside the mother's body. In many species the unborn young behave as cannibals and feed on other unborn sharks within the mother's body.

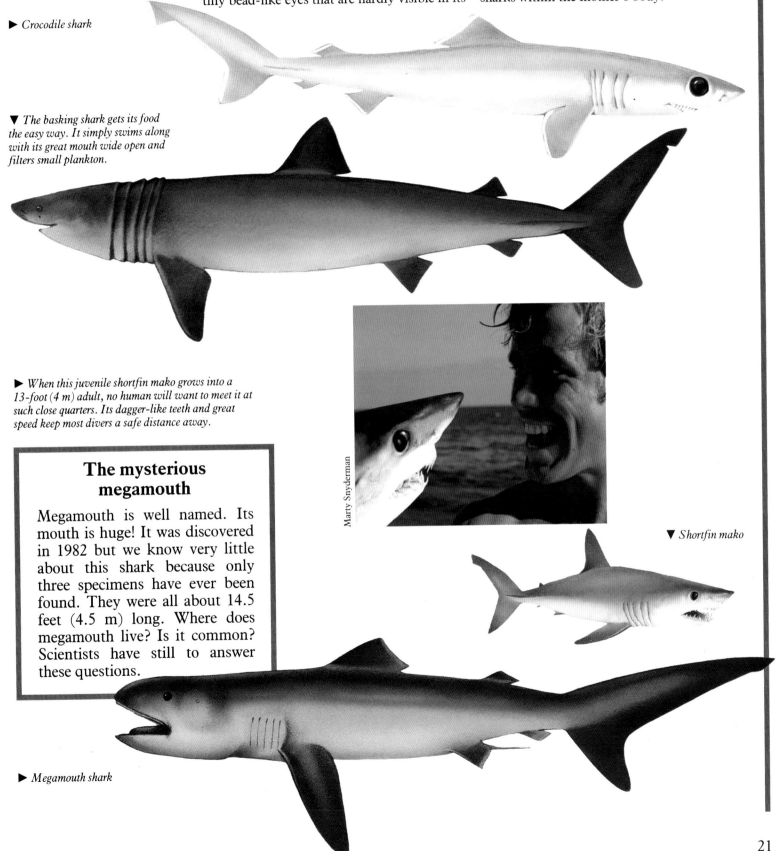

▶ *Crocodile shark*

▼ *The basking shark gets its food the easy way. It simply swims along with its great mouth wide open and filters small plankton.*

▶ *When this juvenile shortfin mako grows into a 13-foot (4 m) adult, no human will want to meet it at such close quarters. Its dagger-like teeth and great speed keep most divers a safe distance away.*

Marty Snyderman

▼ *Shortfin mako*

### The mysterious megamouth

Megamouth is well named. Its mouth is huge! It was discovered in 1982 but we know very little about this shark because only three specimens have ever been found. They were all about 14.5 feet (4.5 m) long. Where does megamouth live? Is it common? Scientists have still to answer these questions.

▶ *Megamouth shark*

## 8 Groundsharks
### (Order Carchariniformes)

Almost 200 of the 350 known species of sharks belong to this group. They are particularly numerous in the tropics and are also common in cooler and deeper waters.

More than 90 species belong to the species known as catsharks, so named because their eyes resemble those of cats. All of them are small, most growing to less than 2 feet (60 cm) long. The swellshark, however, is one of the largest catsharks, and can grow to 3 feet (1 m) long.

Like the catsharks, houndsharks live in coastal waters and do not venture far out into the oceans. Some, however, live at depths of more than 6500 feet (2000 m).

All species of houndsharks produce live young. The tope shark can have a litter of up to 50 young and has been known to live for as long as 50 years.

Houndsharks generally remain on the sand, mud or rocks of the seabed, where they find the shellfish and other invertebrates that are their main food. Some species also eat large numbers of bony fishes.

◄ *Swellshark*

▼ *Tope shark*

Catsharks generally live on the bottom of the ocean in deep coastal waters and most of them, including the swellshark, lay eggs from which the young hatch. Other catsharks produce litters of up to 10 young.

Another large family is the houndsharks. There are 34 species of houndsharks. The largest of them, the tope shark, can grow to about 6 feet (1.8 m) long. This shark is very good to eat and is also popular for its liver oil.

◄ *The pelvic fins and claspers of an Australian swellshark. Although male sharks have two claspers, only one at a time is inserted into the female during mating.*

Neville Coleman

◄ *A tope shark pup. Litters of these sharks can range in number from six to more than fifty.*

Weldon Trannies

You would certainly recognize a hammer-head shark if you met one, although you might find it hard to distinguish between some of the nine species that belong to this family. Four of them can grow to more than 10 feet (3 m) long and the largest, the great hammerhead, can reach almost 20 feet (6 m) in length.

The most common sharks in the world belong to the 48 species that make up the family known as whaler sharks. The sharks that are most dangerous to humans, including the much-feared tiger shark and the blue shark, are members of this family.

The blue shark is found in more parts of the world than any other shark. It is easily recognizable by its bright blue color. Like many other members of this family it ranges far out into the oceans, but stays near the surface of the sea.

The blue shark can produce litters of more than 100 young.

Ron & Valerie Taylor

▲ *A side view of a great hammerhead, a massive and menacing predator.*

▶ *Bull shark*

▶ *Great hammerhead*

▶ *Blue shark*

Another whaler shark you should not get too close to is the bull shark. This shark is unusual because it can live for a long time in fresh water and often travels great distances up rivers. It is not fussy about what it eats and will eat other sharks, including quite large ones, and even younger members of its own species. It will also eat dead animals and is known to be a man-eater.

# Sharks large and small

This page shows illustrations of eight sharks, ranging from one of the smallest to the very largest. Many people believe that all sharks are large and dangerous, but this is quite wrong. Most sharks are not very large at all. On average, sharks are about 5 feet (1.6 m) long, and most of them are 3 feet (1 m) or less. Even if a shark is large, this does not mean that it is dangerous. The two largest sharks, the whale shark and the basking shark, are quite harmless to humans. In fact, the whale shark is quite curious and friendly and often lets divers ride on its back.

▲ *The great white is a powerful marine predator.*

Ron & Valerie Taylor

▲ *A diver hitches a ride on a whale shark.*

Ben Cropp

**Q.** Do tiny sharks feed only on animals smaller than themselves?

**A.** No. One of the smallest sharks is the cookiecutter shark. When fully grown it can be held in the palm of a hand. It often attaches itself to larger marine creatures, such as whales and dolphins, and uses its sharp teeth to bite off pieces of flesh.

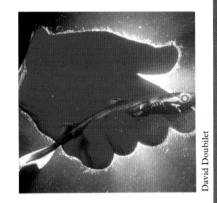

David Doubilet

*Cookiecutter shark*

*Pigmy ribbontail catshark 9 inches (0.24 m)*

*Piked dogfish 5 feet (1.6 m)*

*Port Jackson shark 5.5 feet (1.6 m)*

*Ornate wobbegong 9 feet (2.9 m)*

*Bull shark 11 feet (3.4 m)*

*Great white shark 21 feet (6.4 m)*

*Basking shark 26 feet (7.8 m)*

*Whale shark 45 feet (13.7 m)*

# Where do sharks live?

Sharks live in all the world's oceans. Many swim in warm tropical waters, while others prefer the freezing cold water of the Arctic and Antarctic. Some swim near the surface and others spend all their time far down in the ocean depths.

### Top and bottom

Many sharks are very active. They often cruise in search of food and sometimes they will lunge at their prey with a great burst of energy. These sharks usually live in the upper parts of the ocean.

Other sharks, however, are much more sluggish. These are the bottom-dwelling sharks that spend most of their time on the sea floor. Among the bottom-dwellers are the catsharks, angel sharks and wobbegongs. They often sit, camouflaged, on the sea bottom, waiting for a meal to come past. When they sense something coming, they dart out, catch it, and then wait for something else to turn up.

But some of the bottom-dwelling sharks do move around quite a bit. These are the larger nurse sharks, zebra sharks, and tawny nurse sharks. They all grow to between 10 and 14 feet (3 and 4 m) long, and can swim strongly in their search for food.

### Along the rivers

The bull shark swims in both fresh and sea water. Sometimes called the freshwater shark, it has been recorded in the Mississippi River in the United States, the Amazon River in South America, the Ganges River in India, the Congo River in Africa, and the Brisbane River in Australia. In the Amazon, it has been seen 4500 miles (3000 km) away from the sea.

It is very dangerous to humans. Sometimes it attacks pilgrims bathing in the Ganges, India's holy river.

▼ *The whitetip reef shark lives among the coral reefs of the Pacific Ocean. During the day it rests in caves. It spends most of its time near the bottom, often as deep as 130 feet (40 m).*

### Cold water sharks

Although most sharks live in fairly warm water, there are some that prefer the icy water near the Arctic and Antarctic regions. The Greenland shark, for example, has been found swimming under the ice near the North Pole. Other sharks live in the cold waters of the ocean depths. Below 1000 feet (300 m), even tropical waters are freezing cold. One species, the Portuguese dogfish, has been seen swimming 5000 feet (1500 m) below the surface. These sharks probably swim great distances because food is hard to find at such depths. However, we do not know much about them because the ocean depths have not yet been fully studied.

### Migration

Every year, some sharks move from place to place in a definite pattern. They migrate to follow changes in the water temperature, as most sharks do not like water to be too hot. In winter they are happy near the equator, but when the weather warms up and the sea temperature rises, they follow the ocean currents farther north and south to cooler and more comfortable waters.

Many of the smaller sharks, however, occur only in limited areas. The Tasmanian spotted catshark, for example, is found only around part of the island of Tasmania, while the Japanese dogfish lives only in the waters around Japan.

▶ *The nurse shark is often found resting on the sea bottom.*

Ron & Valerie Taylor

**Q.** Which shark holds the record for long-distance travel?

**A.** The blue shark is the long-distance traveler among sharks. Sharks tagged near Long Island, New York, have been caught again near Spain, and others tagged off the coast of England have been found in the waters of Brazil and New York.

▼ *The Port Jackson shark is a bottom-dweller and is usually found in quite shallow water.*

Jeff Rotman

Esther Beaton/Auscape

# Relatives, friends, and enemies

Sharks are closely related to another group of marine animals — the rays. Like sharks, rays have cartilage in their skeleton instead of the bone that distinguishes the bony fishes. There are about 470 species of rays. Among them are stingrays, mantas, cow-nosed rays, skates, guitarfish, and sawfish. They all have flat bodies and long tails.

We have already seen that many sharks are good swimmers and excellent hunters, and other sea creatures take advantage of these skills. Small pilot fish can often be seen swimming close to a shark, whose shape and movement make swimming easier for them, and as a result they often get scraps of the shark's leftover food. Sucker fish or remoras sometimes hitch a free ride by sticking themselves to a shark with a suction disk on their head. The remoras are like a clean-up brigade and are often found inside a shark's mouth or on other parts of its body, where they eat *parasites* such as worms, leeches, and tiny shellfish that feed off the shark.

There is no doubt that people are sharks' worst enemies. A shark has much more chance of being attacked by a human than a human has of being attacked by a shark. Many millions of sharks are hunted and killed by humans every year — many for food, some for "sport." In an average year, on the other hand, sharks injure only a dozen or so people, and only two or three attacks may result in death.

▲ *The common Australian stingray has a painful sting in its tail. It often lurks in very shallow water and can catch fishermen and other "paddlers" unawares.*

▼ *Although remoras often attach themselves to sharks, they can swim strongly on their own.*

▶ *The guitarfish is a ray that spends much of its time partly buried in sand on the seabed.*

Jean-Paul Ferrero/Auscape

Jean-Paul Ferrero/Auscape

Ned Middleton/Seaphot

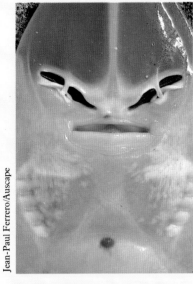

▲ *A close-up of the gills and nostrils of a guitarfish.*

▶ *A large stingray lies partly buried in the sand while a lemon shark swims above it. Lemon sharks are large, active hunters that eat a wide range of prey, including small rays. But a ray as large as this need have no fear.*

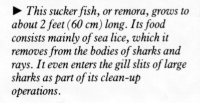

▲ *Copepods are tiny shellfish that sometimes infest and live off the fins and gills of sharks. They are often called "sea lice."*

▲ *A brightly colored coral shrimp busy at work, cleaning parasites from the skin of a wobbegong as the shark lies on the sea bed.*

▶ *This sucker fish, or remora, grows to about 2 feet (60 cm) long. Its food consists mainly of sea lice, which it removes from the bodies of sharks and rays. It even enters the gill slits of large sharks as part of its clean-up operations.*

# Food for sharks

Many people believe that sharks will eat anything that comes their way. Some sharks are like this, but others can be very fussy eaters!

Most of the larger sharks are *carnivores*, or meat and fish eaters. They generally prefer fresh food to meat that is already dead. But one shark, 11.5 feet (3.5 m) long, caught near Sydney, Australia, was reported to have all these things in its stomach: eight legs of mutton, half a ham, the front half of a dog, the back half of a pig, as well as 297 pounds (135 kg) of horsemeat. All this must have been dumped at sea!

Many kinds of sharks are very particular about what they eat. Some feed on small fish and squid; others prefer sea urchins and shellfish. The sicklefish weasel shark is very fond of octopus. Some sharks like to eat baby sharks or pups, either of their own kind or another species.

Other sharks though will eat just about anything that turns up. The tiger shark is one of these — it has been called a trash can with fins! — and this is one reason why the tiger shark can be so dangerous to human beings.

Some sharks change their diet as they grow older. Young shortfin mako sharks, for example, feed on small fish and octopus that they catch and chew with their long pointed teeth. When the sharks are older, these teeth are replaced with sharper and wider teeth so that they can catch and break up bigger animals such as dolphins, seals and sea lions.

The cookiecutter shark has a very strange feeding habit. It attaches itself to a whale, a dolphin or another shark with its strong lips, then uses its small but sharp teeth to bite out a plug of flesh. Sometimes the cookiecutter gets confused and attaches itself to an underwater cable or perhaps the rubber-coated parts of submarines. This mistake causes quite a lot of expensive repairs and certainly doesn't satisfy the cookiecutter shark's appetite.

The nurse shark, which lives on the ocean floor, gets food from cracks and holes in rocks and coral. It puts its thick lips over the hole and sucks up its food rather like drinking through a straw.

◀ *A blue shark swims among a feast of squid. When they find a feast like this, the sharks will cruise through the water with their mouths open, and eat until they can fit no more into their bodies.*

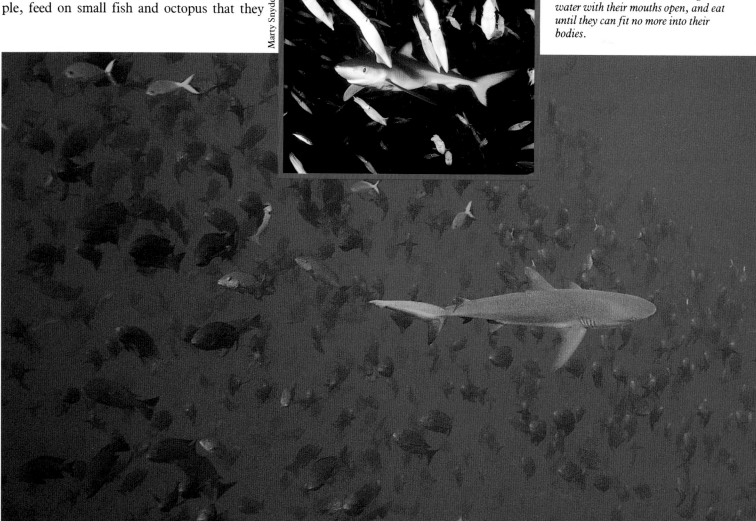

Marty Snyderman

Jeff Rotman

David Doubilet

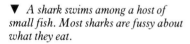

▲ *The sharp even teeth and strong lips of a cookiecutter shark.*

▶ *If they are excited by blood or chemicals in the water, sharks sometimes lash about in a feeding frenzy. When this happens, they will eat almost anything that comes their way.*

▼ *A shark swims among a host of small fish. Most sharks are fussy about what they eat.*

## Catching food

The largest sharks — the whale and basking sharks — have unusually small teeth. Unlike most sharks, their mouth is right at the front of their body. These sharks cruise slowly near the surface of the water with their mouths wide open. Every hour, more than a thousand tons of water pass through the shark's mouth. Thousands of tiny *plankton* — minute plant or animal particles — are caught in the gill rakers, and the water then drains out through the gill slits.

Some sharks have unusual ways of catching food. The thresher shark uses its long tail as a club to hit and stun fish. The sawshark uses its sharp, saw-like teeth to slash out at its prey and cut it up.

Most sharks seem to eat every day or two, although they can live for several months without eating.

Edward S. Hodgson

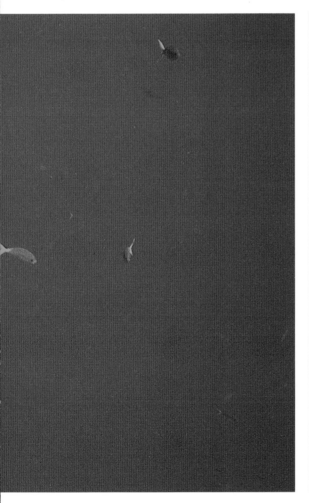

## How a shark solved a murder case

**VITAL CLUE**

◆

Tattoo Marks On
Man's Arm

———

**POLICE SEARCH**

IF the police succeed in establish-
ing by fingerprints, the identity
of the victim whose arm was
disgorged by a shark in the Coogee
Aquarium Baths last week, the feat
will be an even greater triumph
than that achieved in the now
famous human glove murder at
Wagga.

In the country crime, the experts
performed almost a scientific miracle
and to do it had to make a glove of
skin from the murdered man's hand.
    The case of the arm found at Coogee
presents difficulties, because the tissues
of the hand skin have been practically
destroyed.
    However, C.I.B. experts believe that
a print can be secured.
    Detective Sergeant Keogh, who is in
charge of investigations with Detective
Sergeant Young and Detectives Man-
ion and Head, is also hopeful of estab-
lishing identification through the tattoo on the inside of the arm.
    It is a fairly crude bit of work and
depicts two boxers in fighting stance.
    Detective Sergeant Keogh would like
to hear from anybody who can remember a man possessing such a tattoo.
    Many theories are being investigated
including murder and suicide.
    After investigating the lists of mis-
sing men police have failed to find
anybody described as having a tattoo.
    The Government Analyst's report
which is awaited will disclose whether
the limb was amputated at a hospital
operation and by some way found a
last resting place in the sea.

In April 1935, near a popular beach in Sydney, Australia, a fisherman caught two sharks with one line — a small, half-eaten shark and the huge tiger shark that was eating it. He towed the tiger shark to the beach and handed it over to an aquarium.

A week later, the shark spat out a human arm that had a tattoo clearly visible on it. Dr Victor Coppleson, a shark expert, was called in to study the arm. He concluded that it had not been bitten off by the shark. Whose arm was it? How did it get there?

The police published a photograph of the tattoo and it was not long before a man identified it as that of his missing brother. Investigations followed and the police arrested two men for the murder of the missing man. They believed the men had cut up the body, stuffed it into a trunk and dumped it in the sea. The arm would not fit, so it was tied to a weight and thrown into the sea. It had stayed intact inside the shark's stomach for at least eight days and probably much longer.

# How do sharks reproduce?

Some sharks reproduce by laying eggs; others give birth to live young. Unlike the eggs of most fish, sharks' eggs are large and well protected, so the young shark has a good chance of surviving.

Most fish reproduce by spawning. The females release their eggs into the sea and the males shed a mass of *sperm* on top of them. The sperm enter the eggs and fertilize them. The fertilized eggs divide again and again, and begin to grow. This is a very simple way of reproducing, but it is also very wasteful. The unprotected eggs and *larvae* face many dangers before they are large enough to protect themselves. Although thousands of eggs are laid, only a few will survive to become adult fish.

Sharks have developed more efficient ways of reproducing. Instead of laying millions of eggs, they produce fewer, bigger eggs. Each one contains food to keep the developing shark, or *embryo*, alive. To make the chances of survival even greater, the male shark places the sperm inside the shark's body. This is called internal fertilization.

**Mating**

Male sharks have a pair of claspers, which become longer and harder as the shark grows. When the male and female sharks mate, one clasper is put into the female's body. Sperm, which have been produced in the male's body and stored in a duct or sac, flow from the male, along a groove in the clasper, into the female's egg chamber, or *oviduct*. Seawater is squirted out to help the sperm make the journey from the clasper into the oviduct.

The bodies of many female sharks are marked with cuts and scars. These tooth nicks or "love bites" are part of the male's courtship behavior. They let the female know that the male is ready to mate as well as helping the male to hold on to the female while they are mating. Perhaps this is why female sharks have much tougher, thicker skin than males.

▼ *Four stages in the development of an oviparous shark, in this case the swellshark. The eggs are laid in greenish cases, and take about ten months to hatch. As the embryo develops it feeds on the yolk inside the egg, which gets smaller as the young shark grows. When it is ready to hatch, it forces its way out of the egg case and immediately begins to swim in search of food.*

A. Kerstitch/Seaphot

A. Kerstitch/Seaphot

A. Kerstitch/Seaphot

A. Kerstitch/Seaphot

Eric M. Le Feuvre

▲ *Mating between sharks is rarely observed by humans. Mating can take between ten seconds and two hours, depending on the species.*

▼ *The egg case of the draughtboard swellshark is attached to seaweed.*

After mating, the sperm are stored in the female's shell gland for up to a year. When the female's eggs are ready, they burst out of the ovary and are swept down to the shell gland where the sperm are stored. The eggs and the sperm join together, and the life of a new shark begins.

Each fertilized egg is stored in a specially made egg case. Egg-laying sharks produce tough, hard cases to protect the eggs as they develop on the sea floor. Sharks that give birth to live babies produce thin egg cases like clear plastic. The fertilized eggs grow in these cases inside the mother's body.

## Did you know?

Did you know that some sharks are cannibals? Thousands of eggs grow inside the mother's body. The first group to hatch survives by feeding on the unhatched eggs that the mother keeps producing. Oddly, we know very little about how the great white shark reproduces, because a pregnant female has never been caught and studied.

## Egg-laying sharks

Some sharks are *oviparous* — they lay eggs. Among the oviparous sharks are most of the 92 species of catsharks, some of the carpet sharks and all eight species of bullhead sharks. When the eggs have been fertilized, the female deposits them, in their egg cases, on the sea floor. Here the embryo develops, nourished by the yolk inside the egg, until the baby shark is ready to hatch.

Some egg cases have tendrils and underwater "cables" that wind around seaweed, the stems of underwater plants, or even underwater cables to anchor them. In the case of the crested bullhead shark, which is found only in Australian waters, these tendrils can be as much as 6 feet (1.8 m) long. The egg cases of the Port Jackson shark, and of some other bullhead sharks, are tough and leathery and spiral-shaped. The female shark sometimes carries these egg cases in her mouth and uses her snout to push them deep into holes or cracks in the rocks to protect them. They stay there, safe from other sea creatures, until the shark pups are ready to hatch from the eggs.

Oviparous sharks usually lay their eggs in pairs and some sharks lay up to 25 eggs in one year. They take several months — sometimes even up to a year — to hatch into baby sharks. The time needed for hatching is long in cold temperatures and shorter in warm water temperatures.

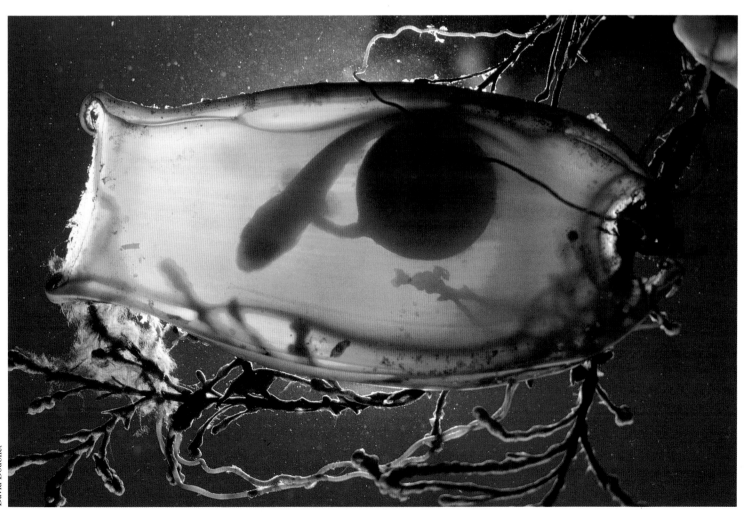

David Doubilet

### Viviparous sharks

Scientists believe that ancient sharks were oviparous. But as sharks have evolved, more and more species have become *viviparous*. This means that the eggs develop inside the female and are all stored in separate compartments. While they are developing, the embryos feed from the yolk in the egg and sometimes from extra food supplied from the mother's body. Some species of sharks produce only two babies at a time. The sand tiger, for example, gives birth to two pups, each of which is almost half as big as the mother shark. The blue shark, on the other hand, can produce up to 100 pups at once!

When they are ready to survive by themselves (usually after nine months or a year), the baby sharks are born. The piked dogfish has a pregnancy of 22 months — the longest known pregnancy of any shark. At the end of this time it produces about ten pups, which are 10 inches (25 cm) long. Young sharks that develop inside an adult female are generally better protected than those that hatch out of eggs on the ocean floor. But once the babies are born, the mother does not help them to survive. This is a dangerous time for baby sharks, because they are often caught and eaten by other sea creatures, including some species of adult sharks.

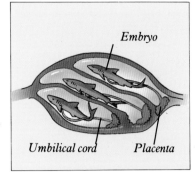

▲ *In viviparous sharks, each unborn shark develops in a separate compartment in the mother's uterus.*

David Doubilet

◄ *During mating it is common for the male shark to bite the female and produce the kinds of scars that can be seen here. Female sharks have developed thicker skins than males, and this helps them from being seriously hurt by these bites.*

▼ *A diver helps a captured lemon shark give birth to one of its litter.*

David Doubilet

▶ *Divers hook the captured lemon shark so that they can observe it giving birth to its pups.*

David Doubilet

David Doubilet

▲ *Each pup rested for a short time after its birth.*

▶ *The newborn shark swims away. As it goes, the umbilical cord will snap and the shark will be free of its mother. The baby shark now looks after itself, because the mother takes no further interest in it. Notice the sucker fish, or remoras, hovering around the large shark. As each new pup was born these fish moved in and ate up the placenta.*

David Doubilet

## The birth of a litter

The photographs on this and also the previous page show the birth of a lemon shark pup. An 8½ foot (2.6 m) pregnant female lemon shark was captured near Bimini in the Bahamas so that scientists could study her. It was the first time that a shark was observed giving birth in its natural environment. So that she could not escape, the shark was attached to a boat by a hook in her mouth.

Lemon sharks belong to the family known as "requiem" or "whaler" sharks. All 48 species in this family give birth to live young. During the pregnancy of a whaler shark a protective skin, called a *placenta*, develops around the embryo in the mother's uterus. The unborn shark receives nourishment from the mother through a tube called an umbilical cord — just like a human baby. When the pup is born the placenta floats away in the water, and the umbilical cord breaks as the young shark swims away.

The shark in these photographs produced a litter of ten pups. Each pup was about 2 feet (60 cm) long. Nine of the pups seemed healthy and normal. The last one to come out of the mother was born dead.

# feeling

Sharks are well equipped to hunt for food and keep out of danger. They have good senses of touch, hearing, taste, smell, and sight. As well, they have one quite remarkable sense — the ability to detect electrical impulses in the water.

## Touch and hearing

A shark's ability to feel and hear depends on tiny cells, rather like hairs, near the surface of its body. Most of these cells are in canals along a line called the *lateral line*. You can see from the diagram that the lateral line extends from the shark's head right along its body to the tip of its tail. Messages about the outside world are passed from the cells along this lateral line into the shark's nervous system.

Cells inside the shark's ears or lateral line pick up vibrations and pass the information through the nerves to the shark's brain. Experiments have shown that sharks are especially sensitive to low-frequency sounds.

## Detecting electricity

The shark's most remarkable sense is its ability to detect electrical currents. This helps them in many ways. For example, the animals they are hunting may give out electrical impulses,

**Q.** Can sharks learn?

**A.** Yes. They can learn in about the same way that rats learn in a laboratory. Nurse sharks have been trained to pick objects up in their mouths and to come when they see and hear certain signals. They can be taught to press buttons to get food.

▼ *Sharks, especially active hunters like this sand tiger shark, have keen eyesight and a well-developed sense of smell. The sand tiger's nostril is divided into two sections by a flap of skin. Water flows into the nostril on one side of this flap, and out again on the other side.*

Kevin Deacon/Auscape

which the shark can follow. Being able to locate electrical impulses also helps sharks to keep their balance. Studies show that the shark's ability to locate electricity is better than that of any other animal.

To locate electricity, sharks use sense organs in their snouts. You can see the openings to these in the photograph on this page. They are tiny holes, or pores, in the shark's skin. The diagram shows where these sense organs are located and also how they are linked to the lateral line.

Scientists believe that sharks' ability to find electrical currents may also help them to navigate in their long swims across the ocean and through the earth's magnetic field. Sharks may sense weak electrical fields and use them as a compass. They may follow these magnetic fields, year after year, as they migrate from place to place.

## Putting it together

Imagine a shark, cruising the ocean in search of food. From a long distance away, it may hear the struggles of an injured fish or pick up the vibrations sent out by a possible source of food. As it swims closer, it may pick up a smell — perhaps it is blood from the fish. This smell will help the shark move closer to its prey. Some sharks will criss-cross the trail; others follow the trail straight toward the fish.

When the shark is close enough, its senses will pick up electrical impulses — perhaps from the beating heart of the fish. Then the shark may circle around its prey, watching it closely. It may prod it with its snout to find out what it feels like. Then, it goes in for the kill. A thin skin closes over its eyes and the gills work overtime to provide an extra burst of energy. The jaws open and close and the shark lunges. Another meal has been found.

▶ *The lateral line extends from the snout right to the tip of the tail. The red lines in the bottom diagram show the lateral line canals in a shark's head. The dots show the position of the holes that allow sharks to sense electrical impulses. The close-up of a shark's head shows the tiny pores that lead to the sense organs.*

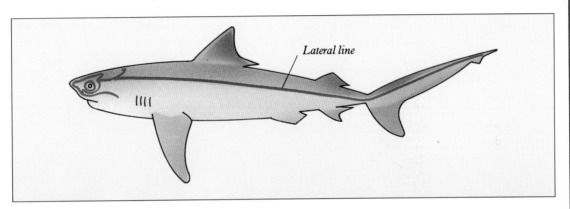

Lateral line

Neville Coleman

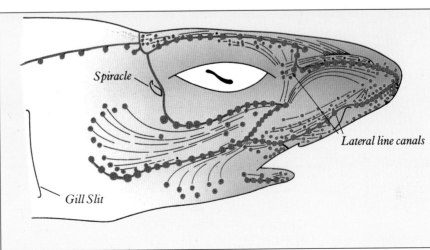

Spiracle

Gill Slit

Lateral line canals

# Eyes and nostrils

The size and shape of a shark's eyes depend very much on where it lives. Sluggish sharks such as hornsharks and carpet sharks have tiny eyes; they probably do not rely on sight very much to catch their prey. More active sharks have bigger eyes and the largest eyes of all belong to the thresher shark. Its eyes look upward, probably to help the thresher see the prey it will club with its long tail.

Many people think of a shark as a "swimming nose." In many ways this is true because sharks have a good sense of smell. Their nostrils are usually found toward the front of the snout, just in front of the mouth. Inside the nostrils are folds of tissue and inside this tissue are the cells that pass messages about smell to the shark's brain. As the shark swims, water passes through these cells, so the shark is always aware of any changes in the smell of what is around it.

Ron & Valerie Taylor/Australasian Nature Transparencies

▲ *The position of the hammerhead's eyes, at opposite ends of its snout, give it a wide range of vision.*

◄ *The large eye of a blue shark. Like many other sharp-sighted predators, the blue shark has a layer of plates behind its retina, which reflect light, rather like a mirror. This greatly improves the shark's ability to see in the water.*

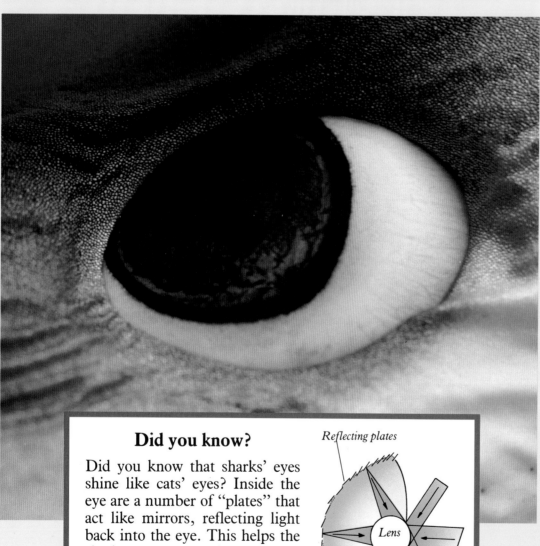

Ron & Valerie Taylor

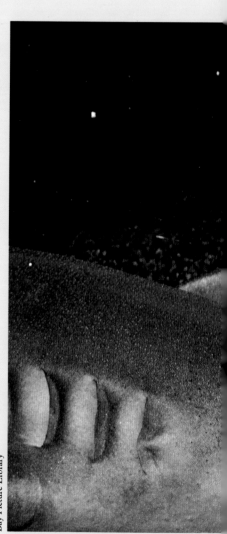

Bay Picture Library

## Did you know?

Did you know that sharks' eyes shine like cats' eyes? Inside the eye are a number of "plates" that act like mirrors, reflecting light back into the eye. This helps the shark to see more clearly. If the shark is swimming in bright, shallow water, the "plates" can be darkened just as a curtain can be pulled across a mirror.

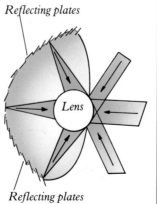

*Reflecting plates*

*Lens*

*Reflecting plates*

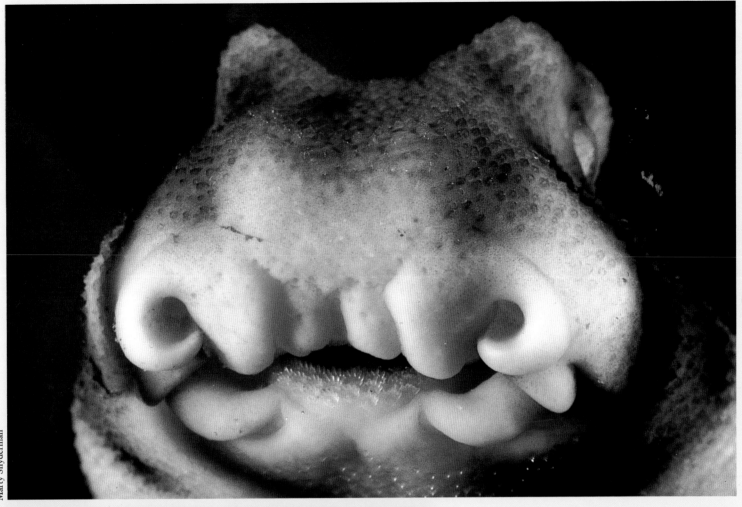

Marty Snyderman

▲ *The large and sensitive nose of the Port Jackson shark helps make up for its poor eyesight.*

◀ *The nurse shark's nostrils are situated at the tips of its wide snout.*

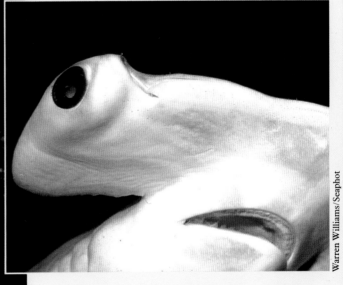

Warren Williams/Seaphot

▲ *Hammerhead sharks have good vision, a strong sense of smell and well-developed electrical senses.*

39

# Why sharks attack

Books and movies often show sharks as prowling, dangerous man-eaters that will attack without reason and eat anyone who gets in their way. But is this true? Here we look at what researchers have discovered about why sharks attack people.

Many shark attacks occur so suddenly that victims and bystanders are unable to observe clearly just what took place, or even what kind of shark was involved. Researchers have suggested different ideas or theories about the reasons for shark attacks.

### Attacking for food

It is often assumed that when sharks attack humans they are looking for food. Many people even believe that sharks swim around looking for humans to eat. But if we study what has actually happened during recorded shark attacks, it seems that the sharks involved would probably have behaved very differently if they had really wanted to eat their victims.

A study of 1200 recent shark attacks in different parts of the world showed that in three out of every four cases the shark bit or lunged at its victim only once or twice and did not try to "go in for the kill." If the shark had been determined to eat the person, it would probably have done so.

### Mistaken identity

Another possibility is that in many cases, but certainly not all, the attacking shark mistakes its victim for a large fish or a seal. When it realizes its error, the shark may swim away without continuing the attack.

Many attacks have been recorded on surfboards and small boats, and sometimes large chunks have been bitten out of them. No

▼ *Below: The presence of blood and other food in the water can sometimes make sharks seem to go mad. They can become angry and aggressive and bite wildly at anything they find. This behavior is called "feeding frenzy."*

▼ *Bottom: People stranded in the ocean are less likely to be mistaken for fish and bitten by sharks if they hunch themselves up or huddle together in a group.*

Ron & Valerie Taylor

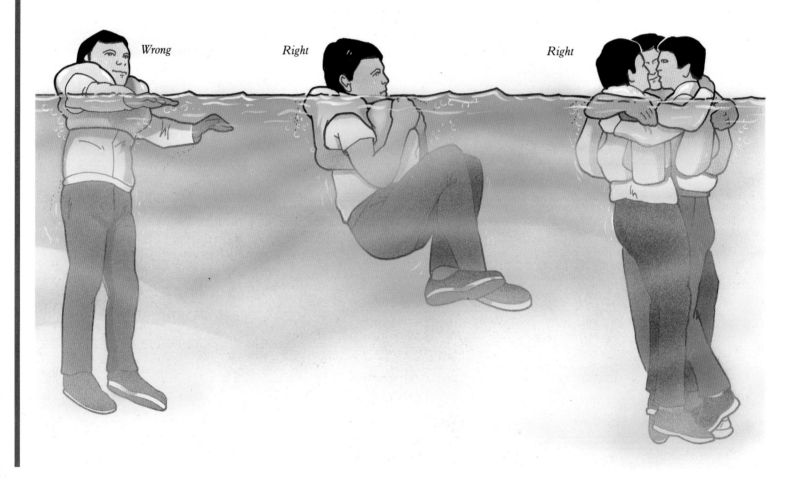

*Wrong*          *Right*                    *Right*

one would suggest that a shark enjoys eating fiberglass, but it is not hard to believe that from below these objects could be mistaken·for large fish or seals. Surfers in wetsuits, too, can at first glance be mistaken for small seals.

### Rogue sharks

During the 1950s an Australian researcher, Dr Victor Coppleson, carried out an investigation into shark attacks and came to some interesting conclusions. He noted that most attacks, at least in Australian waters, were made by sharks that were alone. It was rare for a pack of sharks to attack a human. From this observation, Coppleson developed a theory that became commonly known as the "rogue shark theory."

Coppleson claimed that certain individual sharks, which he called "rogues," were responsible for a series of attacks. He found, for example, that in some places where there had been no shark attacks for many years, a number of attacks would suddenly occur in a fairly short period. Then, as quickly as they had begun, these attacks stopped again. Coppleson believed that the attacks were the work of one of these "rogue sharks."

### Defending territory

Most animals, even normally quiet domestic pets, can become aggressive if another animal invades their territory. A possible explanation for many shark attacks is that the shark is merely trying to drive off a human intruder as it would any other animal that ventured into its space. While some animals can do this by scratching or trampling, a shark's only weapon of defense is its teeth!

### Provoked attacks

If someone had you cornered and you thought they were going to hurt you, you would probably fight back. So do sharks, and it is fairly certain that many attacks on divers or fishermen happen because the sharks feel threatened. A diver who is following a shark or pointing a camera at it could easily look threatening to the shark. Even a person who is bitten while standing in the water near a beach, may have seemed frightening to the shark!

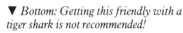

▼ *Below: A great white decided to taste this surfboard. Fortunately the surfer managed to escape.*

▼ *Bottom: Getting this friendly with a tiger shark is not recommended!*

Rich Mula/Ocean Images

Al Giddings/Ocean Images

## Did you know?

When great whites attack people, they usually seem very intent on eating their victim. In this way they are different from other species. But they rarely end up eating the people they bite, who often die from loss of blood or from the injury caused by the bite.

# Dangerous sharks

The three most feared sharks in the world are the great white, also known as the white pointer, the tiger shark, and the bull shark. The coast of California in the United States has the highest record of attack by great whites. Between 1950 and 1982 this region recorded an average of 1.3 attacks a year. However, divers have also reported that great whites have come up and inspected them without making any effort to attack them.

Tiger sharks are found in the warm waters around America, Africa, the Pacific Islands, and Australia. They are strong swimmers and travel over long distances. Their sharp teeth and huge jaws make tiger sharks particularly dangerous. Both tiger sharks and great white sharks grow to 19.5 feet (6 m) long. Tiger sharks have been given their name, not because they are so fierce, but because the young sharks have stripes across their back, rather like those of a tiger, which fade as the shark grows.

Bull sharks are smaller than the tigers and great whites, and grow to about 11 feet (3.5 m) long. Unlike other sharks, bull sharks can live in fresh water. They are the most dangerous sharks in tropical waters, and may even be the most dangerous sharks of all.

► *Bull shark*

## Did you know?

The great white shark is the only shark — in fact, the only fish — that can lift its head out of the water. Among the great white's favorite meals are seals and sea lions. The sharks poke their head out of the water to look for these animals or to scare them so that in fright they jump into the water where they can be caught.

◄ *The gaping jaws of a tiger shark.*

► *Only an experienced and very brave diver should do this with a great white.*

... with the blood of a recent meal, swims toward the cage in which a photographer is sheltering.

Al Giddings/Ocean Images

Distribution of the bull shark.

Distribution of the great white shark.

◄ Great white shark

Ron & Valerie Taylor

Ron & Valerie Taylor

In 1958 the United States Navy established a Shark Attack File at the Smithsonian Institution in Washington. The idea was to record and study all known cases of shark attacks to find out if there were any patterns to them. Researchers compiled a file of about 1200 attacks from around the world, using newspaper cuttings, reports from divers, swimmers and scientists, and the accounts of victims themselves. Although the Shark Attack File was closed in 1967, it still provides the best record we have of shark attacks.

## Shark attacks in Australia

Before the beaches of eastern Australia were protected with nets, Australia had the world's worst record for shark attacks. Since records began, more than 300 attacks in Australian waters have been reported, which represents more than one-quarter of all the attacks listed in the Shark Attack File. However, more Australians are killed as a result of automobile accidents every month than have died in 100 years from attacks by sharks.

## Signs of a threatened shark

Scientists studying gray reef sharks have discovered some interesting facts about what happens when these sharks are threatened by unusual sounds or quick movements. They lift their head and wag their tail, push their front fins down, arch their back, twist and turn, and swim in a series of loops and spirals. When sharks are cornered and feel threatened, they perform this display before attacking.

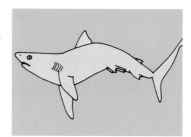

AF Photographic Library

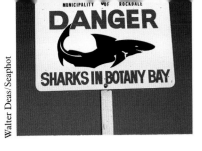

▲ *Signs like this warn swimmers in popular swimming places of the danger they may face from sharks.*

occurred around the east coast. This does not mean that there are more sharks along the east coast — just that many more people live there and swim in the Pacific Ocean during the hot summer months. Eight out of every ten attacks took place between November and March. Almost all the attacks happened between 2 pm and 6 pm — the most popular time for swimming.

Dr Coppleson's research showed that people had more chance of being attacked by a shark if they were swimming alone or in a small group, or if they were on the edge of a large group. Usually, a shark would make two or three lunges at one person and ignore the other swimmers. His studies showed that sharks would attack in clear water or muddy water, in any weather, and at high tide, low tide and in between.

## When do sharks attack?

In the early 1950s Dr Coppleson studied 104 cases of shark attacks in Australian waters. This diagram shows the times at which the attacks happened. As you can see, most of them occurred in the afternoon.

Coppleson also found that in the far north of Australia, shark attacks occurred all year round. In Tasmania, shark attacks occurred mainly in January, which is the middle of summer and the favorite holiday period. In other words, there are more shark attacks when more people are swimming.

► *Distribution of the tiger shark.*

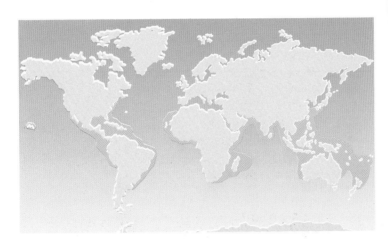

◄ *The blacktip reef shark sometimes attacks divers. It is common near reefs and islands, mainly in shallow warm water.*

► *The great white is fast-moving, aggressive and intelligent — an extremely dangerous enemy.*

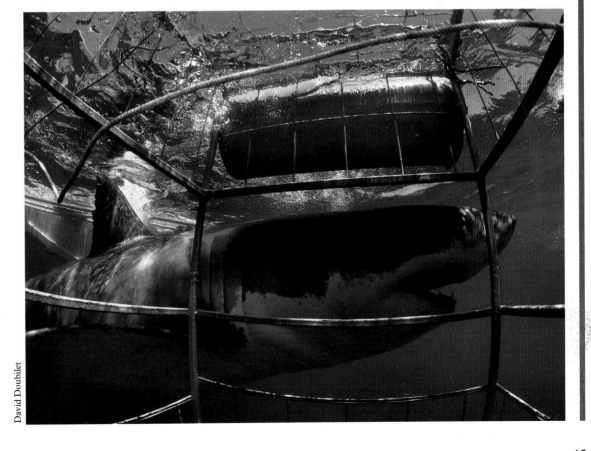

### Shark attacks in South Africa

The map on pages 50–51 shows that, as in Australia and the United States, most of the shark attacks recorded in South Africa have occurred on the east coast. Three-quarters of the South African attacks happened on the beaches of Natal. The capital of Natal, Durban, is a popular holiday resort, and many thousands of swimmers flock there in the summer as the currents are warmer than those of the west coast.

Records show that between 1940 and 1978, there were 69 shark attacks in the waters off Natal. Twenty-five people died as a result of these attacks. Most of the attacks took place before a shark netting program began in South Africa. There have been very few attacks since the mid-1960s.

**Q.** What is the most dangerous beach in the world?

**A.** Amanzimtoti, 17 miles (27 km) south of Durban in South Africa, has the world's worst shark attack record. There have been 11 attacks since 1940, three of them fatal. Nets were placed off the beach in 1962, but there have been six attacks since then!

Tim Storer

▲ *During the summer months thousands of surfboard riders are attracted to beaches in many parts of the world. Shark attack is one of the hazards of this popular sport.*

◄ *Bull shark*

## Sharks and sardines

At a certain time every year, huge schools of sardines migrate through the waters of Natal. When this happens, the Natal Sharks Board takes up all the shark nets so that the sharks, dolphins, rays and large fish that follow the sardines do not get tangled in the nets and damage them. During the sardine run, the beaches are closed until the nets are put in place again.

At least 100 species of sharks swim in the waters off the coast of South Africa, and in most cases, it is difficult to say exactly which species was responsible for particular attacks. However, four sharks known to have injured or killed humans in South African waters are: the great white, the tiger shark, the oceanic whitetip, and the bull shark. Of these, the great white and the bull shark have been blamed for most of the attacks.

Oceanographic Research Unit

◄ *Installing shark nets off one of the beaches in Natal. Almost 50 of Natal's beaches are now protected by nets like these.*

▲ *This sign at a beach in Durban warns swimmers about the dangers of shark attacks in both English and Afrikaans.*

▼ *A swimmer might have become a victim of this 10-foot (3 m) tiger shark if the beach had not been protected by nets.*

Although the bull shark is smaller than the great white, it has large teeth and jaws, and often swims close to the shore.

Shark fever hit the beaches of Natal in 1957–58. In five months there were seven shark attacks and five of these were fatal. Four of the attacks took place in one month — "black December, 1957." Panic grew to fever pitch in April 1958 when there were two fatal attacks. People cut short their holidays and left the seaside resorts. The beaches were suddenly deserted.

The owners of hotels, resorts, shops, and restaurants became worried about the drop in their business. First, they tried building sharkproof pools, but these were too expensive. Ships of the South African Navy were then sent to drop depth charges out at sea to kill the sharks. In fact, very few sharks were killed, but large numbers were attracted by the dead and stunned fish, so local policemen went out in small boats to throw hand grenades on the sharks cruising for food in the area.

In the early 1960s local councils began installing nets to protect their beaches and in 1964 they joined to form what is now called the Natal Sharks Board, which organizes all the netting programs in the area. The Board builds and repairs the nets, and keeps the equipment in good order.

## The attack on Damon Kendrick, February 13, 1974

Damon Kendrick was 14 years old and a keen surfer. He and his friend Joe were training for the lifesaving championships when Damon was attacked by a shark at Amanzimtoti beach in Natal, South Africa. Swimming had been banned in the area because the shark nets had not been checked for several days. The sea was murky and visibility was poor. Damon tells what happened:

> Joe was about 16 feet (5 m) away from me when he suddenly shouted. As I turned, a shark bit my leg and I heard a growl as its powerful jaws shook me viciously . . . Everything took place so fast that I really didn't know what was happening. The shark shook me for about two seconds and as it let me go I was pushed into the shorebreak, which washed me on to the sand . . . Only then did I know what had happened and my mind did not want to accept what I was seeing. Great strips of skin and muscle hung like old rags from where my calf muscle used to be. Blood spurted and dripped from my leg.

Damon had been bitten three times. His injuries were so bad that his leg had to be amputated below the knee.

### Shark attacks in the United States

Americans have 50 times more chance of being struck by lightning than of being attacked by a shark. In the whole of the United States, there are fewer than 12 shark attacks each year.

Three-quarters of the shark attacks recorded from the United States on the Shark Attack File were from the east coast. The other attacks were mainly in California, which attracts millions of swimmers and divers in the summer months. The waters off the Californian coast may be the home of the world's biggest number of great white sharks. The Shark Attack File showed that almost 40 per cent of attacks by great whites took place in the waters of a 125-mile (200 km) stretch of beach in California.

Many of the patterns that have been found in Australia are also true of the United States. Most attacks occur in the middle of the afternoon in summer, in depths of between 5 feet (1.6 m) and 10 feet (3 m). This is because there are more swimmers in the water in these conditions, and so more chance that a swimmer will get into the territory of a shark. People who are bleeding or splashing about noisily are more likely to be attacked than others. Divers carrying speared fish are another target because the fish are food for the sharks.

### Shark attacks in the Pacific

It is hard to tell how many shark attacks have occurred around the Pacific Islands. Sharks and shark gods are an important part of some island cultures and as most Pacific Islanders are familiar with sharks they do not have the same fear of them as people who live in other places. There are very few written records of shark attacks, mainly because many of the islands are so remote.

The Shark Attack File lists 189 attacks in the Pacific area (including New Zealand), most of which have occurred around Hawaii and Papua New Guinea. The most southerly attack in the world happened in 1962 when a man swimming in waist-deep water at the bottom tip of the South Island of New Zealand was bitten on the wrist.

▼ *This diver seems unaware that he is about to have company!*

Terry Kerby/Ocean Images

▼ *This illustration, which was published in 1906, shows a shark attack near Guyana, on the east coast of South America. The men on the raft are escaping through shark-infested waters from the dreaded prison on Devil's Island.*

## Did you know?

More than 2000 years ago the Greek philosopher Aristotle wrote a book called the *History of Animals*. Aristotle claimed that because sharks' mouths were underneath their heads, they had to turn their backs on their prey before they could eat it. He believed this was Nature's way of stopping them from eating too much.

### Shark attacks in other places

The first recorded attack by a shark was noted by the Greek historian Herodotus nearly 2500 years ago. He described how a Persian war fleet was destroyed when the sailors were "seized and devoured by monsters." A later historian wrote about "fierce fights with the dog-fish" in the Mediterranean Sea. He described how the fish attacked "all the white parts of the body." The Shark Attack File lists 18 attacks in the Mediterranean between 1863 and 1961. No attacks have been recorded since then.

The northeast coast of India has a bad record for fatal attacks. Bull sharks, which are known to swim into rivers, have attacked pilgrims bathing in the sacred Hooghly River near Calcutta. They may have been attracted by bodies dumped into the river. Three hundred years ago one traveler in India wrote that people who were "weary of this world" threw themselves into the river "to be devoured of these Fishes."

Millions of sharks are caught by fishermen each year and some of the attacks listed in the Shark Attack File have occurred when sharks have fought back. The world's most northerly attack took place in Scotland in 1960, when a small shark, caught in a fish net, bit a fisherman on the arm as he was dragging the net on to a trawler. The usually gentle basking sharks have also been known to smash boats and injure people when they were harpooned for the oil in their livers. These kinds of attacks by threatened sharks are called "provoked attacks."

### The shark callers

Pacific Islanders have learnt to use the shark's sense of hearing to attract them. Fishermen in the Solomon Islands, Tonga, Fiji and other islands make rattles from cane and disks cut from coconut shells, which they dangle in the water. They know that the sound made by the rattling is similar to that of a struggling fish. Sharks are attracted to the shell rattles, which helps the fishermen to catch them.

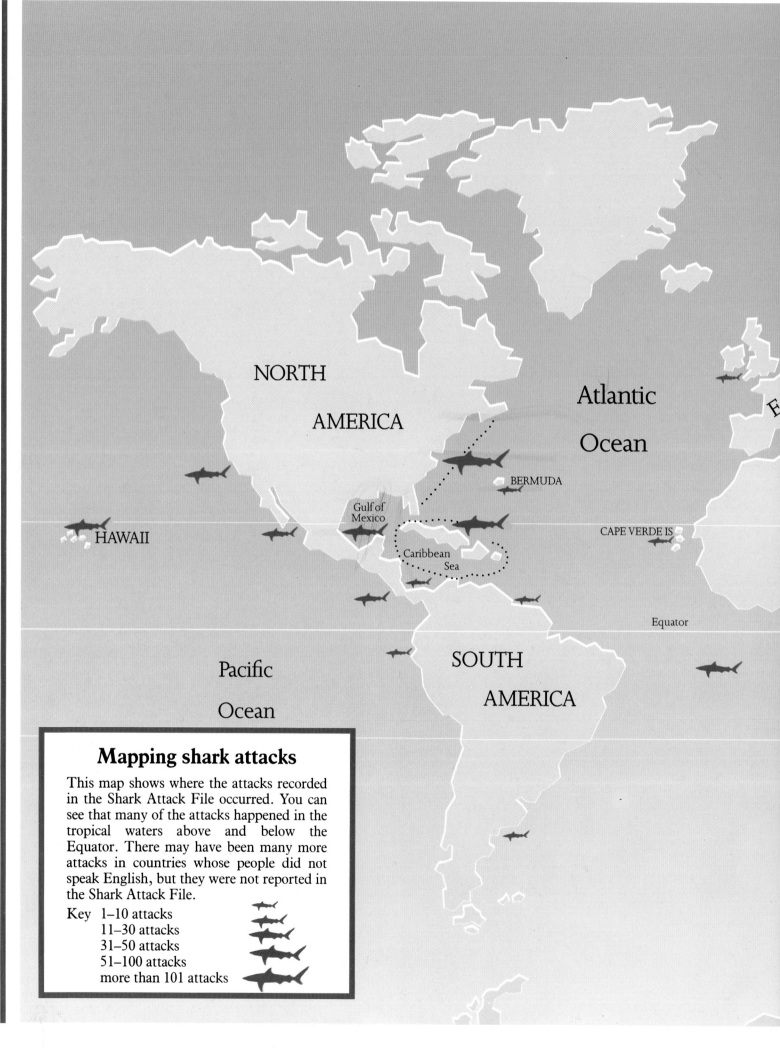

NORTH

AMERICA

Atlantic

Ocean

E

BERMUDA

Gulf of
Mexico

HAWAII

CAPE VERDE IS

Caribbean
Sea

Equator

Pacific

Ocean

SOUTH

AMERICA

## Mapping shark attacks

This map shows where the attacks recorded
in the Shark Attack File occurred. You can
see that many of the attacks happened in the
tropical waters above and below the
Equator. There may have been many more
attacks in countries whose people did not
speak English, but they were not reported in
the Shark Attack File.

Key  1–10 attacks
     11–30 attacks
     31–50 attacks
     51–100 attacks
     more than 101 attacks

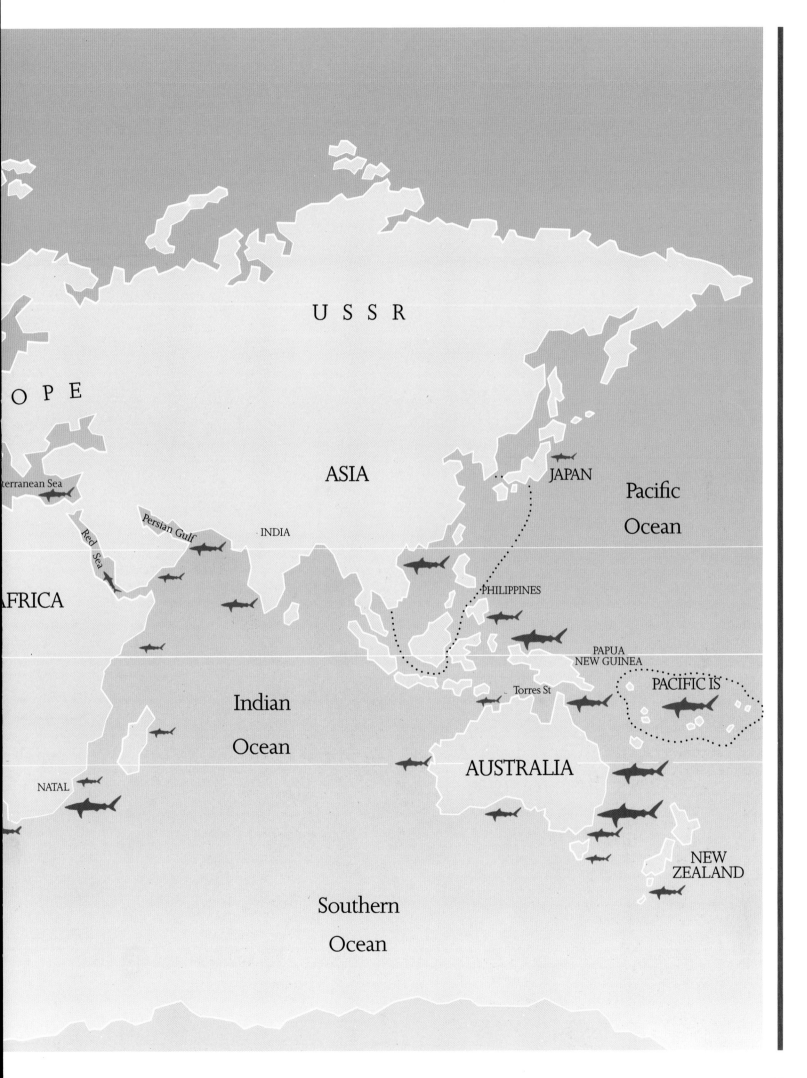

USSR

OPE

ASIA

JAPAN

Pacific

Ocean

terranean Sea

Persian Gulf

Red Sea

INDIA

PHILIPPINES

AFRICA

PAPUA
NEW GUINEA

Torres St

PACIFIC IS

Indian

Ocean

NATAL

AUSTRALIA

NEW
ZEALAND

Southern

Ocean

# Legends about sharks

People have always created legends out of creatures that terrify them. Beasts of prey figure in many of the world's most famous myths and legends. Think back to the fairy tales you were told as a small child, and you will remember that real and imaginary animals like bears, wolves, and dragons played a large part in making them exciting and sometimes frightening.

### Mystery and terror

Sharks have always been mysterious and terrifying. Even today, when we have found out so much about the animal world, we still have a great deal to learn about the way sharks live and behave.

The myth that sharks are hostile animals with a thirst for human blood has been helped along by the kind of publicity that shark attacks receive in newspapers and on television. This myth has been strengthened by the exaggerated treatment of sharks in some sensational movies. We seem to like creating and believing legends about terrifying crea-

tures that we hope we will never meet at close quarters. The reality, however, is that even people who often swim in the sea are much more likely to be injured in a car crash, or bitten by a poisonous snake or spider, than to be attacked by a shark.

▲ *This drawing of a man being attacked by sharks was published in Italy in 1555. Is the huge ray coming to the man's rescue or is it coming to help the sharks finish him off?*

▼ Watson and the Shark, *John Singleton Copley's famous painting, was first shown in 1778.*

*Watson and the Shark*; John Singleton Copley; National Gallery of Art, Washington; Ferdinand Lammot Belin Fund

### Sharks in movies and paintings

The movie *Jaws* burst upon the screen about fifteen years ago. For some years it was the biggest money earner in the history of films and it certainly helped to make popular the image of sharks as terrifying monsters. But sharks had been getting a bad press much earlier than that. More than 200 years ago the famous American painter John Singleton Copley painted a dramatic picture that was supposed to show a shark attack that actually happened in Havana harbor. Although it is a highly exciting painting, and full of action, the shark does not really look like any known species and its size has been exaggerated. The victim, Brook Watson, who seems about to be eaten whole in the painting, in fact lost a foot in the attack. He later became the Lord Mayor of London.

Accounts by sailors often referred to sharks that followed their ships, presumably in search of human flesh. In fact the sharks were really attracted by scraps of food that were thrown overboard.

▼ *The artist who painted this picture for the cover of* Time *magazine could never have seen a shark quite like this one — except perhaps in a nightmare.*

TIME

**SUPER SHARK**

'Jaws' on Film and Other Summer Thrillers

### Pictures true and false

Some of the scenes in the movie *Jaws* were filmed off the coast of South Australia. Filmmakers spent weeks training great white sharks to leap out of the water and attack the chum they had hanging from their boat.

But some of the scenes that had people sitting terrified on the edges of their seats did not involve real sharks at all. What people saw was film of three cleverly constructed mechanical models, which were operated by 13 technicians. These models — all called Bruce — were almost 3 feet (1 m) longer than any known great white and had greatly oversized teeth. They certainly looked real enough!

## Sharks and Australian Aborigines

Sharks have featured in the mythology of many places in the world, especially in societies where people lived close to the sea. Australian Aborigines frequently represented sharks in their cave and bark paintings. According to one Aboriginal legend, the red color of some rocks on an island off the north of Australia was caused by the blood of a dolphin-man who had been attacked by a tiger shark in the seas nearby.

Aborigines also realized the value of the oil in sharks' livers as a source of nutrition, and in their paintings of sharks they sometimes highlighted the liver with extra color to indicate its importance to them.

## Shark legends of the Pacific Islands

It is not surprising that sharks are more important in the myths and legends of the Pacific Islands than in those of other cultures. Most islanders live very close to the sea and depend upon it for their survival. Many of them earn their living as shark fishermen. Even those with other jobs often meet and have to cope with sharks.

In some Pacific cultures sharks are worshipped like gods and considered to be human. The following story was told by a man from the Solomon Islands:

All the fish that are in the sea here we can eat — sailor fish and boar fish and sea slugs and bonito and trevally and barracuda. Dolphins too. But not sharks. Sharks are human. To us a dolphin is just like another fish. A dolphin is not a shark . . . We never fish for sharks. He is a person with us.

Is it safe for you to swim in the sea? Yes it is safe . . . Here you are protected. What happened was that a long time ago a shark, the one that my tribe follows, came out of a woman. The woman gave birth to the shark . . . Ever since then my people worship the shark, and the sharks stop attacking people in the lagoon. The spirit of that woman entered into the shark, therefore when we worship the shark we are worshipping the

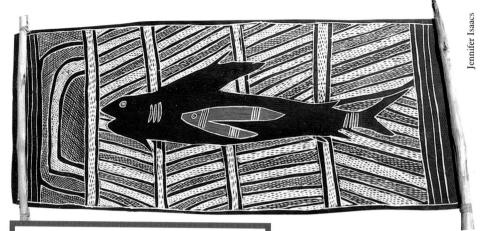

*Jennifer Isaacs*

▲ *This Aboriginal bark painting from Arnhem Land, in Australia's Northern Territory, uses an "x-ray" technique to illustrate the shark's liver, which the Aborigines knew to be rich in oil.*

---

## Goodies and baddies

In most Pacific Island legends, sharks are shown to be good and helpful to humans, but a legend from Hawaii tells another story. People who create trouble in the village are described as sharks that have been turned into human beings. Some Pacific Islanders reflect their fear of sharks in a myth about a shark god who destroyed everyone who dared to venture into his cave.

---

old people. We talk to them when there is a sacrifice.

Oh the sharks come right in, almost onto the beach. The last time we called the sharks everyone was there, we were all in the water with the sharks, talking to them and patting them on the back. Nobody was harmed.

Yes, the priest still makes the sacrifice. He sacrifices to all the sharks . . . We call to all the sharks that come here. The white shark, the black-tip shark, the gray reef shark, the shark-like-the-whale, the hammerhead shark, the tiger, the shark-with-no-proper teeth. They are familiar to us, we never eat them. We adore them.

▶ *A Pacific Islands shark god, in human form. The statue is carved in wood and stands just over 15 inches (39 cm) tall.*

◀ *A shark spirit, carved into a cuttlefish shell.*

*Brian Brake/Auckland Institute and Museum*

# Catching sharks on film

For more than twenty years sharks have figured in some very popular movies. Filming many of the scenes for these movies involved the filmmakers in real-life adventures and often placed camera operators and film crews in hair-raising situations. Many of the photographs in this book, too, were taken by people who had to be resourceful and courageous to obtain them.

▲ *Part of a training session for one of the real great whites that starred in the movie* Jaws.

### Problems for shark photographers

When photographers want to get still or moving shots of dangerous land animals, they generally do not need to be face-to-face with the animals they are photographing.

Taking photographs underwater is a different story. Even in conditions that are almost ideal, you cannot get a good sharp picture of a shark, or any other sea creature, if you are more than about 10 feet (3 m) away from it. If you are farther away than that, the water will always create a blurred effect, and getting close is again important because many sharks are naturally colored to blend in with their surroundings.

### Getting sharks to cooperate

Working up enough nerve to get close to sharks while handling delicate and sometimes complex cameras and equipment is something that comes with practice. Often the really hard part is getting the sharks to stay close enough to you.

The photographer, then, must give the shark a good reason to stay close by. If you want to get a really dramatic shot of gaping jaws and sharp teeth, you have to provide something for the shark to bite.

Underwater photographers generally use bait for this purpose. The bait is called "chum" and using it is called "chumming." Many normally slow-moving sharks are spurred to swift action by the prospect of food, but sometimes, in their excitement, they can mistake the photographer for the food! Shark photographers must always be alert.

### Protection

Steel cages are the best form of protection for underwater photographers, especially against the larger and more dangerous species of sharks. But these cages are very difficult to keep steady in rough conditions and, as the photographer is trapped inside, he or she cannot go after the best shots.

The Neptunic sharkproof suit, which is described on page 62, gives photographers reasonable protection and still allows them to move around in the water in their search for great photographs or heart-stopping footage. If, in the excitement of it all, a photographer does get in the way of a sharp set of teeth, he or she should be protected enough to survive to see the resulting film — provided, of course, that the shark is not a 2000-pound (900 kg), 20-foot (6 m) monster.

▶ *Horsemeat is used to lure this great white shark near a cage where a photographer waits, hoping for some great action shots.*

◀ *The closer you get, the better the portrait. This blue shark seems curious about this strange intruder and his complicated equipment.*

# Using sharks

In many ways — more than you would imagine — sharks are very useful to human beings. Among other things, we use them for food, medicine, cosmetics, ornaments, and jewelry.

Ben Cropp

▲ *The tiger shark is a species much sought after by big-game fishermen.*

### Sharks as food

For thousands of years sharks have provided people with a valuable source of food. In many countries today fish and chips, bought from the local seafood shop, is a popular meal, and the fish sold is very likely to be one of several species of shark, even though it may be called "skate" or "dogfish."

In Chinese cooking shark fins have been treated as delicacies for centuries, and in ancient Greece and Rome shark flesh was regularly served at the best banquets. Sharks today form part of the staple diets of people as diverse as the Lebanese, Vietnamese, West Indians, Indonesians, and Sicilians. Even French chefs have recently been creating mouth-watering new dishes based on shark.

### Shark oil

The livers of sharks are rich in oil, and this oil has been used for many purposes. In some isolated communities where other resources were not available, it has been used as a fuel for heating and lighting.

Because shark oil contains large amounts of Vitamin A, which is important for human sight, scientists are investigating the possibility of using shark's liver oil in human food.

A chemical called squalene, which is present in high proportions in the livers of many species of sharks, has several commercial uses. Many cosmetics and skin creams contain this chemical and it is also used in the manufacture of some medicines and drugs. Squalene was discovered in 1916.

◄ *How people use sharks.*

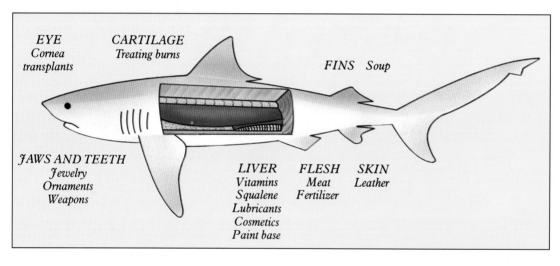

EYE
Cornea
transplants

CARTILAGE
Treating burns

FINS   Soup

JAWS AND TEETH
Jewelry
Ornaments
Weapons

LIVER
Vitamins
Squalene
Lubricants
Cosmetics
Paint base

FLESH
Meat
Fertilizer

SKIN
Leather

▼ *Sharkfin soup, a favorite Chinese dish, but not to everyone's taste.*

Shufunotomo

▲ *Real shark teeth used in a carved wooden ornament.*

**Q.** How have sharks been useful in human surgery?

**A.** In the United States the corneas from the eyes of sharks have been used for human cornea transplant operations. The cornea is part of the outer covering of the eye that protects the pupil. Sharks' corneas have proved to be successful substitutes for human corneas when these are not available for the transplant.

### Shark skins

Because sharks are covered with rough scales, or denticles, it was only recently that their skins were widely used as a source of leather. About seventy years ago researchers in the United States discovered a process by which these denticles could be removed without damaging the shark skin. The skin could then be tanned to produce leather that was even stronger than that made from cattle hides.

High-quality shoes and other clothing are now made from shark skins.

In Morocco shark skins with the denticles still attached are used to produce a tough, very shiny leather known as "baroso." Before modern sandpapers and glasspapers were developed, dried shark skins proved very useful for polishing and planing wood.

### Medical uses

Heart disease is one of the greatest killers in Western societies and today much research is directed at ways of preventing heart attacks. The liver oils of some sharks, especially the deep-sea dogfishes, are thought to contain ingredients that can lower blood cholesterol levels and help prevent blood clotting. These are being closely investigated and may soon prove of great value in the constant fight against human illness.

### Ornaments

Sharks' teeth are frightening while they are still in a shark's mouth, but when they have fallen out or been removed from a dead shark, they have been used to make decorations, ornaments and weapons. Polished, painted and even gold-plated sharks' teeth are much in demand as pendants and other items of jewelry. Whole sets of jaws are popular as wall decorations, and mounted sets can sell for large sums of money.

► *How a shark's skin is removed.*

▼ *Dogfish sharks, like this longnose spurdog, contain liver oils that have many commercial uses.*

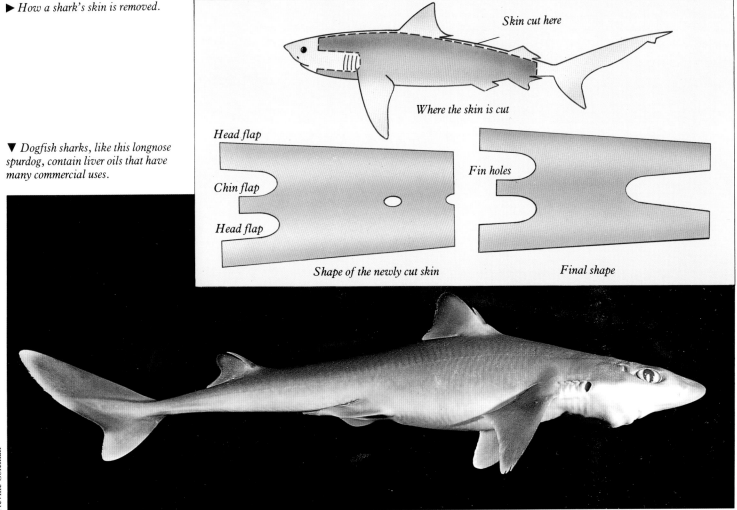

Skin cut here

*Where the skin is cut*

Head flap

Chin flap

Head flap

Fin holes

*Shape of the newly cut skin*

*Final shape*

# Keeping sharks away from people

The only sure way of keeping sharks and people apart is to stay away from the oceans where sharks live. Although shark attack is not a great danger for swimmers and divers, scientists have worked out some interesting ways of keeping sharks away from people. Different methods are needed for swimmers at beaches, divers in deep water, and the survivors of a plane crash or victims of a shipwreck.

### Protecting beaches

The best way of keeping sharks away from people at beaches is by building solid walls or fences in the sea. People can swim safely inside these sharkproof pools while the sharks are kept outside. But these pools are expensive to build and even more expensive to maintain. They are often damaged by storms and high seas and, as they rust and rot in salt water, they

▲ *Caught in the net.*

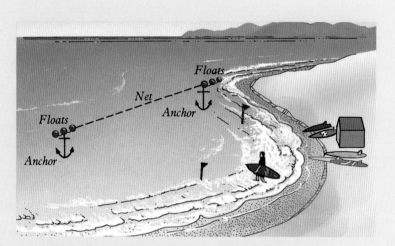

## Protecting beaches with shark nets

The diagrams show how shark nets are put in place to protect swimmers. Each end of the net is secured by an anchor and its position is marked by glass floats, which also help to keep the net upright. The loosely hanging nets, about 20 feet (6 m) deep, are set by people working from skiboats or trawlers. They are usually put down in the late afternoon and hauled up again within a day or two to check the catch.

Netting began in New South Wales, Australia, in 1937. In recent years, about 350 sharks have been caught in the nets each year. Most of these are hammerheads. After a series of deadly shark attacks in South Africa, a netting program was started there in the 1950s. Today, 46 South African beaches are protected by nets. Between 1978 and 1984, more than 8000 sharks were caught in the nets. Most of them were harmless to humans, although the nets did snare great whites, hammerheads and tiger sharks as well.

▲ *The carbon dioxide dart.*

must be constantly inspected for holes and damage. Once there is a hole in a sharkproof pool it is no longer a safe place for swimming.

Meshing or netting is another way of protecting popular swimming beaches. This method is used in South Africa and Australia. Two lines of mesh nets, each about 400 feet (120 m) long, are stretched out in the sea about 1500 feet (450 m) away from the beach. When sharks swim in to the shore, they become tangled in the nets and suffocate as they struggle to free themselves.

Netting has been quite successsful in protecting beaches. But, like other ways of keeping sharks away from people, it is expensive, so only some beaches can be netted. One sad side effect of netting is that many harmless sharks, as well as large fish and other sea creatures, are also trapped and often killed in the nets.

Another way of protecting swimmers, which makes use of the fact that sharks are very sensitive to electrical impulses, has been tested in South Africa. Cables are laid around beaches, and pulses of electric current are sent through the cables. If the electric current is strong enough, sharks will turn and swim away. Researchers spent many years developing this system, but the costs were so high that it is not yet being used.

## Protecting divers

Divers need a form of protection that they can carry with them while they are underwater. It must be reliable, light and easy to operate. In the past, divers have used knives and spearguns to protect themselves from sharks. However, knives are often too blunt to cut through a shark's tough skin and spearguns can be more dangerous to the divers themselves than the sharks.

Explosive hand-spears called bangsticks can protect divers from single sharks. A metal rod with a firing pin at one end is fitted with a powerhead or shotgun shell that explodes when it strikes the shark's body. A good shot can kill a shark up to 10 feet (3 m) long, and even a bad shot will shock a shark into swimming away.

Another hand-held device is a carbon dioxide dart. If the dart is shot into a shark, the carbon dioxide flows through the shark's body and forces it to the surface of the water, where it dies. Frogmen of the United States Navy carried these darts when they were involved in the splashdowns of Apollo space missions.

Some divers carry a thick wooden club called a "shark billy." One end of the club has nails sticking out of it, and the diver uses this to push sharks away. There is also an electrified version of the shark billy.

▼ *A cage is probably the safest place to be when you're underwater with a great white.*

## Suits of armor

Because weapons such as knives, spearguns, bangsticks and gas darts are often more dangerous to divers than sharks, scientists have found other ways of protecting divers. One is an electric shark shield, powered by batteries, and built into the diver's wetsuit. Like the South African cables, these devices contain an electric field that confuses a shark's senses. However, the devices are bulky and uncomfortable to wear, and some divers have complained that the electrical pulses make the fillings in their teeth ache!

One of the most efficient ways of protecting divers is a modern version of the medieval knight's suit of armor. The Neptunic chain mail suit is made from thousands of tiny stainless steel rings linked to make a suit that is flexible enough for the diver to move comfortably. It weighs only a few pounds and provides good protection from even quite large sharks. A bite may still cause a bruise, but the shark's teeth cannot get through the steel mesh.

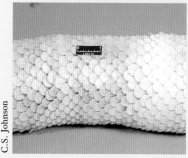

▶ *A powerhead can help divers protect themselves against dangerous sharks such as these bronze whaler sharks.*

▲ *Shark Chaser — an idea that didn't work. The sharks were not chased away. Some even seemed attracted by the chemicals.*

▼ *This diver is allowing herself to be bitten on the arm by a 6-foot (1.8 m) blue shark in order to test the Neptunic chain mail suit.*

## Chemical repellents

In July 1945, toward the end of World War II, a United States cruiser, USS *Indianapolis*, was torpedoed and sunk by a Japanese submarine. The survivors were lost at sea for four days and nights, and only 316 of the 1196 men on board were rescued. Up to 100 were taken by sharks as they waited for help to reach them.

This kind of disaster convinced the United States Navy that its sailors needed protection from sharks. Researchers believed that sharks were repelled by rotting shark flesh, so they created Shark Chaser — a repellent made from the main chemical in rotting shark flesh, mixed with black dye to spread out and hide the sailor from the shark. All this was put into a small package and attached to lifejackets.

The only problem was that Shark Chaser did not work! Research after the war showed that it was useless as a shark repellent and it has not been made since 1976. Other chemical ways of repelling sharks are still being tested, but so far none of them has been really successful.

## Staying safe in a plastic bag

One of the simplest but most effective ways of protecting victims of plane crashes and shipwreck from sharks is the Shark Screen. This is a large dark plastic bag, closed at the bottom, with inflatable rings around the top. It folds into a small package weighing about 1 pound (0.5 kg). If a person is stranded at sea, he or she should unfold the package, blow up the rings at the top of the bag and get inside.

Shark Screen seems to work because it covers up the arms and legs, which are the parts of the body often bitten by sharks, and all the shark sees is a large dark shape. If the person is injured, the plastic keeps blood out of the water and this too may help to prevent an attack.

# Studying sharks

As scientists and researchers study sharks more closely, they are learning more and more about these amazing creatures. Many of the old myths and beliefs are now known to be untrue. But how *do* scientists study sharks?

Sharks are, in fact, very hard to study! Their world — the sea — is not very comfortable for humans. As well as this, sharks can move quickly, and many of the larger and more interesting sharks live alone or in small groups. Some species live in remote and isolated places, or deep below the surface of the ocean. And, of course, some sharks are highly dangerous!

Despite all these problems, we have learned quite a lot about sharks by studying them in their natural environment. A tagging program has helped scientists to understand the migration habits and growth rates of several kinds of sharks.

Because it is so difficult to study sharks in the ocean, researchers have built special shark testing pools where they keep sharks in tanks so that they can be observed and tested. But,

even this is not easy. Sharks are often hard to catch and do not travel well. The water in their tanks must be kept pure, and they must be fed carefully to keep them healthy. Even in these shark testing pools, scientists must be careful whenever they go into the water.

Much of what we know about sharks is based on the study of just a few species. Scientists at the Lerner Marine Laboratory in the Bahamas have conducted many experiments with lemon sharks and nurse sharks. Their research has provided a lot of information about sharks' senses.

In addition to experiments that are carried out in shark testing pools, scientists also work in the laboratory. Here they examine parts of sharks under the microscope so that they will better understand how sharks' bodies work and why they behave as they do.

*Scientists study the behavior and biology of lemon sharks in specially built pools (above and below), and in the wild (right). In the top pictures they are observing whether an electric current is effective in repelling sharks.*

# Glossary

| | |
|---|---|
| ANAL FIN | A fin that extends from the underside of many sharks, quite close to the tail. |
| CARNIVORE | An animal that eats only the flesh of other animals. Most sharks are carnivores, as they feed on the flesh of other fish or marine animals. |
| CARTILAGE | A bone-like substance, which is lighter and more flexible than bone. Sharks' skeletons consist mainly of cartilage instead of bone. |
| CLASPER | The tube-like part of a male shark's pelvic fin, which is inserted into the female during mating. Sperm flow through the clasper into the female's body. Male sharks have two claspers, but probably use only one at a time while they are mating. |
| DENTICLE | Sharks' scales are called denticles. They are like teeth, and are thicker and rougher than the scales of most other fishes. |
| DORSAL FIN | A fin that stands upright on the back of sharks and some other marine animals. All sharks have at least one dorsal fin. Many species have two, but one is usually more prominent. |
| EMBRYO | A young animal in the early stages of development. In the case of sharks, embryos may develop inside eggs outside the mother's body or, like most mammals, inside the mother's body. |
| GILLS | Organs that allow oxygen to filter out of water as it passes into the mouth and out again through the slits or openings in the side of a shark's head. Sharks and other fishes breathe through their gills. |
| LARVAE | The young of an animal that is changing from one form to another. Many fishes hatch as larvae before they take on their final shape. Sharks that hatch out of eggs are usually fully formed and not in a "larval" state. |
| LATERAL LINE | A series of grooves that run along each side of the shark from behind the eye to the tip of the tail, and also extend in various directions around the head. Most of the shark's sensitive hair cells are situated in these grooves. |
| LOBE | A section or part. This word is often used to refer to the parts of a shark's tail, which has an upper and a lower lobe. |
| OVIDUCT | A duct or channel leading from the ovary to the outside of a female shark. The eggs move into this duct where they are fertilized by the male's sperm. |
| OVIPAROUS | Egg-laying. Sharks that lay eggs which hatch outside the shark's body are said to be oviparous. |
| PALEOZOIC ERA | The period in the earth's history between about 570 million years ago and 220 million years ago. |
| PARASITE | An animal or plant that lives on and feeds off another animal or plant. |
| PECTORAL FIN | A pectoral fin extends sideways from the lower part of each side of the shark's body, close behind the head. The pectoral fins help sharks to keep their balance and direction in the water. |
| PELVIC FIN | Smaller than the pectoral fins, pelvic fins extend outward from the lower part of the shark's body usually well back, quite close to the tail. Like the pectoral fins, they help control the shark's balance and direction. |
| PLACENTA | A protective membrane, or skin, that forms around the embryos of some sharks after they have been developing for about three months. |
| PLANKTON | Tiny animals and plants that drift in the ocean, usually near the surface. |
| SPERM | Minute cells produced by male animals. They fertilize the eggs produced by females to create new life. |
| SQUALENE | A chemical substance found in the liver oil of many sharks. Squalene is used in the manufacture of cosmetics, as well as drugs and medicines. |
| VERTEBRATE | Any animal that has a backbone. |
| VIVIPAROUS | Giving birth to live young that have hatched from eggs inside the mother's body. Most mammals, and many sharks, are viviparous. |